HOUSING in the PUBLIC DOMAIN: the only solution

HOUSING in the PUBLIC DOMAIN: the only solution

by Peter K. Hawley

Published by
METROPOLITAN COUNCIL ON HOUSING
24 West 30 Street, New York, N.Y. 10001

412

REVISED AND EXPANDED EDITON

Copyright © 1978 by Metropolitan Council on Housing

Library of Congress Cataloging in Publication Data
Hawley, Peter K., 1901-
  Housing in the public domain.
    1. Real estate business—United States.
2. Housing policy—United States. 3. Public
housing—United States. I. Title.
HD259.H38 1978   333.3'3   77-29103
ISBN 0-9601548-1-7

Preliminary edition published and copyright 1976

Acknowledgment

The efforts of those individuals who worked so dili-
gently with me in the writing and production of this
book are greatly appreciated. But we acknowledge as
even more important the efforts of those who organize
and fight every day in the struggle for decent affordable
housing.

Peter K. Hawley

Contents

Foreword   xiii

Chapter **I**   THE HOUSING FAMINE—WHY?   3

Chapter **II**   LANDLORDS HAVE ABDICATED
THEIR RESPONSIBILITIES   6

     IS REAL ESTATE PROFITABLE?   6

     Capital structure of real estate   7

     The varying policies of control and finance
agencies toward mortgage interest   10

     Profit from operations   11

     The MBR fraud (Maximum Base Rent)   12

     Depreciation   18

     Accelerated Depreciation–an example   21

     Abandonment   24

     The economics of abandonment   25

     Arson for profit   30

     Tax shelters (and handouts from the
public treasury)   32

     The history of government subsidized
housing programs   36

     Section 8   37

     *The New York State Urban
Development Corporation*   38

     *The New York City Municipal
Loan Program*   39

     The "shrinking tax base" and the massive
real estate giveaway   39

     Local Law J-51   43

     Local Law 58   44

     Section 421   45

A detailed and perhaps classic example of
the workings of subsidized housing 46

    Mitchell-Lama housing 47

    Manhattan Plaza 48

Federal Pre-emption 60

Why don't more people go into real estate? 67

    *REAL ESTATE CANNOT AND
WILL NOT BUILD FOR LOW-
AND MIDDLE-INCOME PEOPLE* 69

The current housing shortage—
how and why 69

Increase in "Capital Value" and
effect on new construction 70

Interest rates 71

Landlords have priced themselves out of
the low- and middle-income markets 72

Rent Supplements 73

    ROLE OF THE BANKS 74

Domination of the economy 74

The banks and real estate 76

Interest rates and their justification 77

Federal Guaranteed Mortgages 77

Red-lining, block-busting and ghettoizing 79

What should interest rates be? 80

Chapter **III** **HOUSING IN THE PUBLIC DOMAIN:
WHAT DOES IT MEAN?** 82

Housing must be by and for the people 82

How would it work? A People's
Housing Board and Tenant Committees 83

What goes into Public Domain? 84

    Existing housing 84

    New housing 85

How will the buildings in the Public
Domain be run? 85

    Rents 85

    Management and financing 86

    Occupancy, vacancies and priorities 86

    *Rent limitations on private
real estate* 86

Housing is a basic human right 87

Chapter IV   **SOURCES OF AVAILABLE FUNDS** 88

The responsibility is ours 88

Defining our housing needs 89

How much will it cost? 90

    BUDGET OF AVAILABLE FUNDS 91

Budget categories 91

    *THE FINANCIAL
ECONOMIC FRAMEWORK* 92

Land and structure speculation 92

Federal level sources 94

    Debt and costs 94

    The economy and the budget 94

    *Defense, Foreign Aid and
Space Programs* 95

    *Taxes–who pays them and
who does not* 96

    *Rip-off under the guise
of housing* 97

        Federal New Towns Program 97

        Federal Section 235
(Home ownership program) 97

    Federal miscellany–an example 98

Private industry sources:
corporate profits 98

But—the people, how are they doing?   100

New York State level sources   102

The banks and other giants   102

Another State—Arizona   104

New York City level sources   104

    Municipal misbehavior   104

    While deterioration spreads and
    bankruptcy threatens, our city fathers
    continue on their irresponsible course   106

    Real estate taxes   106

    More giveaways–planned and
    already given   108

    Landlords' threats–City's enticements   109

    Tax-exempt properties   109

    New York City subsidized housing–
    assistance to the rich and to real estate   110

    If it is supposed to be good for the
    people, there is always an angle   111

        Medicare-Medicaid   111

        Day-care centers   112

        Free school lunch program   113

        Nursing homes   113

The unemployed: a source of vast wealth   114

    Funds available for housing and other
    needs, by putting the unemployed to work   115

The budget   118

    Budget recapitulation and
    grand total   124

Chapter V   **CONCLUSION**   126

Appendix I: Legislative memorandum on
              MBR (Maximum Base Rent)   128

Appendix II: Manhattan Plaza depreciation schedule   131

Tables

Table

1. An example of capital profits (capital gains)   7
2. Effects of capital gains on the tenant   9
3. MBR/Rent Control increases since 1972—compounded   13
4. MBR components   14
5. "Capital Value" profits made from only component #5 of the MBR formula   17
6. Accelerated Depreciation   22
7. Effect of Accelerated Depreciation on landord's income tax   22
8. Superprofits from the abandonment process   27

Appendix **II**   Manhattan Plaza—Depreciation Schedule   131

Foreword
to revised and expanded edition

Rent each year consumes a larger proportion of our budget, while, at the same time, the quality of our home existence deteriorates. The third of the nation that President Franklin D. Roosevelt called ill-housed is becoming a larger segment of the population, and the amount of decay becomes more pervasive.

To the individual and family suffering with which F.D.R. was concerned now must be added the decay of our central cities and its economic and social impact.

The why of these distressing problems has been asked many times; the answers have been even more numerous. And many of them have been quite accurate—but, alas, too general, too philosophical.

Out of the need to puncture the hot-air balloon of real estate/banking and the engulfing propaganda that emanates from it, we have undertaken an economic study of these operations. We attempt to penetrate to the core of real estate/banking manipulations; to examine the vast profits that real estate/banking make, and the excessive number of instant millionaires thus created. And, of course, we examine the effects on the ultimate source of these profits, the tenants of the nation and the rest of the population, who are not—nor can they be—isolated from this process.

While the locale we have selected is New York City, it is not because these intertwined causes and effects are limited to that particular area. Rather it is because we in the Metropolitan Council on Housing have functioned there as an organization for 20 years and have grown to know it so well. Thus, though the specific materials we analyze are mainly New York City's facts, experiences and laws, they nevertheless apply in their generality to every other community in the nation—however small or however rural—if not today, then tomorrow.

New York City is the largest example, to be sure. By that fact it becomes the concentrated source for the easier extraction of greater and faster profits. Let there be no doubt about the fact that the ripple effect of real estate/banking's successes in New York City will, in due course, reach every city and hamlet, every tenant and homeowner, every worker—white or blue collar— and every professional.

For reasons not too difficult to understand, the tenant movement in the United States has been slow to start, has moved fitfully, exists fragmentedly—each group operating in its own locality—with only the most rudimentary connections with its fellow organizations in other communities. Yet the need for tenant organization—widespread and united—is daily becoming a greater necessity.

That the painful, impoverishing process of decaying houses at ever higher rents may at first be delayed, then diminished, and finally reversed by the united organizations of tenants, is the reason for undertaking this work.

Peter K. Hawley

September 23, 1977

HOUSING in the PUBLIC DOMAIN:
the only solution

Chapter I

THE HOUSING FAMINE—WHY?

In the richest country in the world—in the country which boasts the greatest know-how and best industrial technology in the world—there exists a housing famine! Why?

An estimated 13 million families in this country suffer "serious housing deprivation." In such housing as does exist, the rents in the last two decades have doubled, tripled, and even quadrupled. Why?

Are these "acts of God" over which man has no control—and therefore must suffer their existence?

Clearly not!

Then what is the cause?

Land has been gathered into the hands of an ever smaller group of people and has become a rare, expensive and monopolized commodity.

The total value of real estate, land and structure throughout the United States in 1971 has been estimated at $3.5 trillion.*

In 1972 the total value of real estate in the United States held by individuals (as distinct from being corporately owned) was one trillion, 492 billion dollars. Of this, 15.1% or $225 billion was owned by the richest 1% of the population. The *New York Times* of July 30, 1976, stated that the richest 6%, however, owned 43.2% or $645 billion—almost half of all personally owned real estate.

Financing Real Estate Development, Harry A. Golemon, A.I.A., editor, for the American Institute of Architects. Based on analysis of the Securities and Exchange Commission and the United States Department of Commerce. Published by Aloray, 1974.

4 Housing in the Public DomainHousing in the Public Domain

We do not need to substantiate the fact that landlords can't or won't build needed housing at rents people can afford. Real estate/banking has not only proven it by having (as this is written in 1976) the lowest rate of construction since the Great Depression of the 1930's, but its spokesmen continually maintain that they cannot build for low and middle-income people.

We intend to prove in the following pages that:

1) Real estate/banking is making exorbitant profits.
2) Real estate/banking has already priced itself out of the low- and moderate-income housing market.
3) By the very nature of the economic jungle in which it functions, real estate/banking is not and cannot be content with current or even foreseeable margins of profit.
4) The construction of new housing is not the only way to make profit. They reason: Why build if more money can be made from trading existing housing or collecting federal, state and city subsidies?
5) While this process goes on, housing decays, the population grows, and the ensuing shortage is used as another excuse for rent-gouging.
6) The role of the banks is central to this destructive process.
7) This chain of economic housing destruction cannot be altered by pleas for justice and decency, or appeals to patriotism and civic duty.
8) Solutions can come about only when those intervening forces are brushed aside, for they contribute nothing to housing, but stand in the way of its construction at rents people can afford.
9) Then and only then can people's tax money be used directly to build housing.
10) We need no experts beholden to real estate/banking. A People's Housing Board and Tenants Committees can guide and administer the planning, construction and operation of housing.
11) This is what we call "Housing in the Public Domain"—free of landlords, speculators, banks, bondholders, interest, mortgage payments, and all the other appurtenances of the top-heavy, destructive, real estate/banking structure.

In June 1976, the United Nations held a world conference in Vancouver, Canada, on this very subject. It was called "Habitat" or "The United Nations Conference on Human Settlements." The *New York Times* reported on June 7, 1976:

". . . Members of the conference were working on the drafting of proposed recommendations for national action that included statements favoring public ownership of land, government regulation of land use, expropriation of profits from land speculation and public 'recapture' of increases in land value attributable to public development."

A week later the Conference decided that:

"Land, because of its unique nature and the crucial role it plays in human settlement, cannot be treated as an ordinary asset, controlled by individuals and subject to the pressures and inefficiencies of the market. Private land ownership also is a principal instrument of accumulation and concentration of wealth and therefore contributes to social injustice."

(New York Times, June 12, 1976.)

It becomes clearer and clearer that the private ownership of the land is a distressing phenomenon—not a local aberration or even a nationwide one. It is global. It has reached such horrendous proportions that the United Nations, which has many compelling problems to solve, felt it necessary to call a world conference on this subject.

The Metropolitan Council on Housing, a New York City tenant union, has for years advocated Housing in the Public Domain. In November, 1975, it called a city-wide conference which adopted a program to promote this objective. It is gratifying to find our position endorsed, so to speak, by a United Nations body.

But let us make our case on its own merits.

Chapter II

LANDLORDS HAVE ABDICATED THEIR RESPONSIBILITIES

Is real estate profitable?

The real estate industry's propaganda mill does a very expert job in publicly shedding tears to "prove" its poverty. It cites rising costs and stresses the abandonment of property to make its point. Would you, it rhetorically asks, throw out a good washing machine or automobile except for the reason that it was no longer useful (profitable) to you? This, of course, is sand in the eyes, thrown up to blind us.

So let us take a quick look at the real estate industry and some highlights of the controlling economics.

$$$$$$$ss

Your landlord is not really your landlord or at least not your total landlord. He is the front-man or managing partner for the banks and insurance companies that hold the mortgages.

The owner of a property (other than the individual homeowner) invests 5% to 10% of the purchase price, sometimes even less, and borrows the balance from banks or other lenders, giving them a mortgage on the property as security. The greater ownership, and therefore power, lies in the hands of the banks. This is why we in Met Council, in order to have a clear perspective of who is our adversary, always speak of the industry as real estate/banking.

Capital structure of real estate

The investment of 5% to 10% to control a property worth 10 to 20 times as much is known as "leveraging."

There are, largely speaking, two kinds of profit in real estate: the first, from the operations (rents) of a property; the second, from the sale of the building. Here it should be noted that the real measure of all profits is the income tax—and what profits are permitted to go untaxed. The real estate industry, in this respect, is the most favored type of enterprise.

As the Real Estate Institute at New York University describes one of its courses in the 1976 Fall Catalogue, "This course examines the impact of taxes on real estate investments. It analyzes the various *tax benefits that make Real Estate a tax-favored industry*" (emphasis added). More about this later.

In the tremendous shortage of housing that real estate has brought into being because of its refusal to build new housing at low and moderate rents, rents have been forced sharply upward. Since the capital value of a building is a multiple of its rental income, the upward spiral of rents creates an upward spiral of the capital value of the building, which in turn creates a new upward spiral of rents.

Table 1 provides an example of the enormous profit made in the buying and selling of real estate. The public, of course, is almost completely unaware of the extent of the rip-off.

Table 1   *An example of capital profits (capital gains)*

1.	An owner *buys* a building "worth"	$1,000,000
2.	He *invests* in cash—10% or (more often 5%)	$ 100,000
3.	And borrows on a *mortgage*—90% or	$ 900,000
4.	Let us presume he keeps the building for two years—raises the rents through one device or another (MBR, lease renewal, etc.), and then *sells*, let us say for	1,100,000
5.	Subtracting his buying price (subtract line 1 from line 4) gives him a *profit* of	100,000

(Continued overleaf)

Table 1 (continued)

The profit is "only" 10% above what he
paid for the building, but since
6.   his *cash investment* was only $100,000, and

7.   his *profit* was $100,000
within two years his capital profit on the
sale is exactly 100%. (If he invested only
5%, his profit would be 200%.)

Assuming there was a 20-year mortgage
and payments of $45,000 of principal are
paid yearly (it is included as a cost in
your rent),
8.   he has paid off in principal
($45,000 x 2 years)   90,000

His mortgage at the time of sale is therefore
only
9.   (subtract line 8 from line 3)   810,000

10. He now has cash in two years of
(add lines 6, 7 and 8) $ 290,000

The $290,000 accumulated by the landlord in only two years,
as shown in *Table 1*, is enough to leverage almost three buildings
of the type he originally bought. The table does not include profits
from the operations of the building.

From this example, it is not too difficult to understand how
sharp operators such as Goldman and DiLorenzo, with $10,000 in
capital 30 years ago, "leveraged" it up to *billions of dollars* in real
estate properties, including the Chrysler Building.

It is worth noting that the income tax laws tax this type of
profit (capital gains) at only half the rate of "ordinary" income,
ordinary income being the kind that 95% of our population receives as the rewards of its labor—including the interest on that
part, if any, that it manages to save for the inevitable rainy day.

As will be shown, even this lesser tax is most often not paid
by real estate operators because of the long list of tax shelters
available to them.

But this is only the beginning; there follows a ripple effect.
Higher investment requires higher income; higher income requires higher rents. *Table 2* illustrates this spiral.

Table 2   *Effects of capital gains on the tenant*

1.	The new landlord now has a building "worth" (although he invested only $110,000). He now recalculates all his costs.		$1,100,000
2.	His mortgage interest, say 9½% (it may be much more), is now (990,000 x 9½%)	$94,050	
3.	Previously it was (900,000 x 9½%)	85,500	
4.	Interest "costs" (even though this is a tax deductible expense) are up by		8,550[1]
5.	His mortgage principal payment each year is now	49,500	
6.	Previously it was	45,000	
7.	Principal payment (even though this is a capital gain and not an expense) up by		4,500
8.	Increased "costs"—for these two items alone (add line 4 and line 7)		$ 13,050[2]

[1] In New York City attitudes toward the allowability of interest as an expense in operations vary from agency to agency. In cities with no controls, the landlord makes his own decisions based on that which serves him best. (See page 10, "The Varying Policies of Control and Finance Agencies Toward Mortgage Interest.")

[2] This table is intended merely to show the outline mechanics of this aspect of speculation and is by no means a complete detailing of "how to make a buck on a quick turnover."

In the existing real estate market, it would be a most unusual building that has been sold only once or twice in the last 20 or so years. It is more likely to have been sold and resold 4, 5 or 6 times. So if we take a conservative average of 4 times and multiply line 8 by that much turnover, the increased "costs" become $52,200 (excluding the compounding effect).

The landlord, taking into account the higher price of the building and his larger investment, wants a greater return.

In New York City, the landlord goes to the Rent Control office or the Conciliation and Appeals Board (in rent-stabilized apartments) to demand his increase, claiming to suffer "hardship." In cities where there are no controls, he merely makes the demands on the tenants, facing them with the alternative of eviction.

So, because the previous landlord made, in two years, a capital-gains profit of $190,000 (190%), the tenants are to be required to pay higher rents—as they will again, when the present landlord next sells it to another.

All this usually takes place without improving the property by one iota. On the contrary, it has most likely deteriorated somewhat in this period.

The varying policies of control and finance agencies toward mortgage interest

The author made extensive inquiries into the diverse methods of treating the matter of interest payments by various agencies concerned with housing. He found that the New York City agency that governs the Municipal Loan Fund does permit interest on the mortgage to be included as a cost in the determination of rents after rehabilitation.

He likewise found that interest was permitted by the federal Department of Housing and Urban Devlopment (HUD) in the computation of costs and their relation to the determination of the amount of rents to be set. This covers most federally subsidized and federally insured housing.

Neither the New York City Office of Rent Control, however, which has charge of rent-controlled apartments, nor the Conciliation and Appeals Board (CAB), which oversees rent stabilized units, permits interest paid on the mortgage to be considered as an allowable expense in the computation of hardship applications.

In the discussion with an official of one of these agencies, some interesting points were made. He stated that if interest were allowed, the effects would be unequal and to the disadvantage of the stable landlord who held on to his building and annually reduced his mortgage (and therefore the amount of interest paid by him). His books would show less expense and therefore less or no hardship. On the other hand, the landlords who were mortgaged up to the hilt and who have sold and resold their buildings at profits, each therefore with a higher mortgage, would be able to show higher expenses and be eligible for greater hardship increases.

This would apply also to the owner who, in an upward-moving real estate market, refinanced his building every few years, thereby not only getting new mortgage money for the inflated real estate but also taking out the built-up equity, that is, the money that he had paid in toward the reduction of his mortgage. This, too, would make for higher interest payments and therefore for higher rent demands.

Finally, it would discourage the landlord from holding onto his buildings, and it would encourage quicker turnover of properties than already exists. It would boost rents even higher and become the financial incentive to speculating landlords to indulge in a faster buying and selling spree than even now prevails.

Profit from operations

This is the area of real estate about which landlords are willing to talk. They never talk (publicly, that is) about their capital gains nor the inflated capital structure nor the various devices for increasing income and profits through tax shelters.

But even when they talk about profits from operations it is neither complete nor honest. They do talk about cash-flow, that is, the total that comes in (rents) and the total that goes out (cash expenditures). They talk about increased labor costs and increased fuel costs. These do exist, but they are a *minor* part of the total items that are labeled as costs. And to the extent that they do exist, they have been more than offset by the relentless increase in rents each year under rent control or with each new lease under rent stabilization.

The MBR fraud (Maximum Base Rent)

The major complaint of landlords is that rent controls prevent sufficient profit in their operation of residential buildings.

The present Rent Control Law was enacted in 1943 during World War II, when the economy was geared to the war effort. This act of Congress froze all prices and rents, barred all new civilian construction, and decreed that rationing be initiated in both the manufacture and distribution of food, clothing and other consumer needs.

The Rent Control Law initially had been designed to protect tenants against landlord rent rises and unwarranted evictions. As the federal proclamation read, the law was ". . . to stabilize prices and rents to prevent hardships to persons. . . to protect persons with relatively fixed and limited incomes from undue impairment of their standard of living. . . .

However, even during the period of federal rent control under the Office of Price Administration (OPA), landlords began to demand and get rent increases, and to obtain changes in the regulations. With the end of the war and the closing of the OPA offices, rent control on a federal level was annulled in every state except New York, which, due to the continuing acute housing shortage, voted to continue rent control, incorporating into its state law and regulations all the rulings that had been made earlier at the behest of the landlords during the six years that federal controls had been in effect. The insistent demands of landlords to weaken the law and relax regulations were also incorporated in the New York State law and regulations.

By an act of the state legislature, the Rent Control Law became the responsibility of New York City in 1962. By that time, the law had become substantially weaker in its protection of tenants' rights and had been further nibbled away by rulings, regulations and judicial decisions.

The MBR law was perpetrated by the very landlords who are today demanding that all controls of rents be eliminated. The city and state legislative bodies have consistently responded to the demands of the landlords, while ignoring and diminishing the rights of the tenants.

As one of its provisions, the MBR grants landlords rent increases of up to 7½% each year, depending on how the computer digests the very complex factors placed into it and how it applies them to each apartment and each building.

As the result of a lawsuit brought by the landlords, the court in 1974 ordered the annual across-the-board 7½% increase—without regard to the computer calculations.

The validity of the continuous anguished cries of landlord poverty due to the "unfair" restraints of rent controls can be judged by the table that follows. It calculates the compounded rent increases that landlords have received under the MBR law only since 1972. The various increases received in all the previous years are not included. These pre-1972 increases range from across-the-board legislated increases to "voluntarily" negotiated ones, the increases in the rent of an apartment when tenants move out. To all these are added capital improvement increases, hardship increases, new stoves, refrigerators, and many more. Major capital improvements and equipment increases continue, in addition to MBR.

*Table 3   *MBR/Rent Control increases since 1972–compounded*

Year	Percentage increase in the "collectible" (actual) rent	Cumulative compounded percentage increase	From 1972 base: compounded annual percentage increase
1972	7½%	7.5%	7.5%
1973	7½%	15.5%	8.0%
1974	7½%	24.2%	8.7%
1975	7½%	33.5%	9.3%
1976	7½%	43.5%	10.0%
1977	7½%	54.3%	10.8%
1977	Labor-Cost Pass-Along 7½% (in addition to MBR increase)	65.9%	11.6%

*From table supplied by William Rowen of the New York State Tenant and Neighborhood Coalition.

Note in the right-hand column how the compounding effect sharply raises the percentage of yearly increase. While it is 7½% in the first year of 1972, in the sixth year of 1977, after the labor-cost pass-along, the so-called 7½% increase is actually 11.6% and the cumulative total is 65.9%.

Projecting these increases for just another three years—until 1980—the annual rate of rent increase will be 14.4% and the cumulative total will be 106.1%—since 1972!

The MBR law has a theoretical "ceiling" beyond which rents cannot go. In actuality even the theoretical ceilings can be penetrated under certain circumstances. In addition, the ceilings that are set are changed every two years. Thus in 1974 the ceiling for each apartment was raised by 8.5% and again in 1976 by 22%. In January, 1978, the ceilings are again due for revision; upward, of course.

The Maximum Base Rent law, however, requires the close scrutiny of some of its even more profound aspects, because it computes rents supposedly on the "scientific" basis of the allocation of *costs* and the determination of allowable and therefore guaranteed profits.

Table 4   *MBR components*

Component	% of MBR Formula	
1) Real estate taxes	14.9%	17.6%
2) Water and sewer charges	2.7%	
3) Operations and Maintenance Expense	39.0%	
4) Vacancy and collection loss	1.0%	
5) Return on Capital Value	42.4%	
	100.0%	

(*A Housing Agenda for New York City*, Bales and Puri, a McKinsey Report, page 31.)

Let us examine these for error, duplicity, and distortion of fact:

Components 1 & 2. *Real Estate Taxes and Water and Sewer Charges:* As of the end of 1975, $1 billion 300 million was due New York City in unpaid taxes. These constitute 17.6% of the rent dollar that the landlords pocketed—which amount the tenants paid to them as part of their rents. Pure and illegal profit! And lest one think that only "hard-pressed" landlords do not pay their taxes, Harry Helmsley (of Helmsley-Spear), one of the largest landlords in the United States, stated in the *New York Magazine* (April 14, 1975) that he would not pay taxes on many of his residential properties.

Component 3. *Operations and Maintenance Expense:* This accounts for 39% of the rent dollar. There are probably very few tenants in New York City and elsewhere who haven't experienced one or more of the following:

• Too little heat (or none in many cases) in winter.
• A reduction in the maintenance staff and cuts in maintenance service. In many buildings there is no superintendent at all.
• Broken and unrepaired facilities including plumbing, heating, dark and deteriorated public areas.
• Landlord's unpaid electricity bills that threaten to turn off light in public areas, operation of the heating system, etc.
• Less frequent and, in many cases, no painting.
• Antiquated or defective and dangerous electrical equipment.
• Add your own experiences.

(Each of these items reduces the 39% of your rent dollar that should have been expended for operations and maintenance and again becomes pure profit for the landlord.)

Component 4. *Vacancy and Collection Loss:* This allocates 1% of the rent dollar. In the existing housing shortage, there are practically no vacancies.

Component 5. *Return on Capital Value:* 42.4% of the rent dollar is allowed for this purpose. This is the area of massive swindle. It includes:

a) Allowance for interest on mortgage.
b) Amortization of the mortgage (repayment of the principal).

c) Assessed value of property x equalization rate x 8.5%
(theoretical profit).

d) Real profit.

Let us examine each of these elements of Component 5

a) *Interest on mortgage* is a blatant piece of fakery: The
entire amount of interest paid by the landlord is deductible from
the landlord's income tax as a business expense and therefore is
repaid by the U.S. government and state government as well.
Just what part of the 42.4% is attributable to interest we are not
told.

b) *Amortization of the mortgage.* This too is a fraud. *This is
not an item of expense.* When the landlord makes a payment to
the bank on his mortgage, he reduces his mortgage by that
amount. He therefore builds up his equity in the building by
exactly that amount. It is as if he were putting the money in a
piggy bank to save. This constitutes pure profit. (See An Example
of Capital Profits (Capital Gains) page 8.)

c) *Assessed Value x Equalization Rate x 8.5%:* The assessed
value of a building is roughly 60% of its "value." The landlord pays
taxes on only this sum, that is, when and if he pays taxes. The
Equalized Assessed Valuation fraud was passed in 1970 as part of
the MBR Law. Its effect is as follows: Let us keep as an example
the $1,000,000 building we used earlier. Its assessed valuation is
approximately $600,000 (60%). Using the Equalized Assessed
Valuation (EAV) formula, the EAV value becomes $1,050,631.
(For full analysis, see Appendix I—Met Council document of
February 21, 1974.) Although the landlord *pays taxes on only
$600,000 of assessed value,* under the MBR Return on Capital
Value he *collects from the tenants rent calculated on $1,050,631.*

The EAV is then multiplied by 8.5%, which is the theoretical
profit for the landlord. While 8.5% seems modest in this age of
inflation, the question is, 8.5% of what? Roughly speaking, he
invests, in cash, 10% (in our example, $100,000) of the cost of a
building. Then the EAV is inflated up to ten times the cash
investment ($1,050,631). Then the 8.5% profit is applied to that
bloated figure. Thus it becomes not 8.5%, but ten times 8.5%, or
about 85%! (See Appendix I.) This is the magic of semantics and
obscurantism.

d) The final major fraud is the real profit. (There are very many minor frauds.) As we saw on page 8 "An Example of Capital Profits," the landlord invested only $100,000 cash in his $1,000,000 building. In the world of business, he is entitled to a profit *only on the actual cash he invested.*

At a profit rate of 10% his profit should be $10,000 per year. At a profit rate of 20% his profit should be $20,000 per year. Even at a rate of 30% his profit should be $30,000 per year.

However, applying only Component 5 (Return on Capital Value) to the $1,000,000 building, the landlord's profit is as follows:

Table 5—*"Capital Value" profits made from only Component 5 of the MBR formula* (See table 4.)

1.	Interest on mortgage (actually returned by U.S. government to the landlord because it is fully deductible as a business expense)	$ 85,500
2.	Amortization of mortgage (equity build-up)	45,000
3.	Equalized Assessed Valuation He gets as part of his rent (8.5% of $1,050,631)	$89,303
4.	Landlord pays real estate taxes of $8.18* per hundred dollars on $600,000 of assessed valuation	49,080
5.	By this double standard—namely, by *receiving* the real estate tax part of the rent dollar on the inflated amount and *paying* his real estate tax on the deflated amount—the landlord gets more than he pays in taxes, the sum of (subtract line 4 from line 3)	40,223
6.	So, from *Component 5 alone* (Capital Value) he receives per year on a cash investment of $100,000—*170%* *profit per year!*	$170,723

*In fiscal year 1976-77 the rate became $8.79 per hundred dollars. In fiscal year 1977-78 the rate was reduced to $8.75 per hundred dollars.

Depreciation

Depreciation is the major real estate tax shelter and basis for profit hidden from the public eye. The theory of depreciation should be, and originally was, that an owner of a property shall be repaid by adding to the cost of the product that part of the machine or facility worn out to uselessness in the process of manufacturing his product or delivering his services. In real estate this has been perverted out of all semblance to anything originally intended or even anything that makes justifiable sense.

Depreciation, as used in real estate and under all the tax laws, has no relationship to the real useful life of a building, its condition or even its replacement. Depreciation is merely an unseen method of making profit by calling this non-cash item an expense. It is one of the most important of real estate tax shelters. It converts a real profit into a paper "loss" and thus allows other cash income such as salaries, interest, dividends, etc. to become tax-free.

Depending on its type, the useful life for income-tax purposes of a newly constructed building is about 40 years. The landlord gets back the entire cost of the building from the federal government (state and city as well) by deducting 2½%* of the building's value from his income tax each year.

No cash is expended. Nevertheless, this deduction reduces the amount of his taxable income, so that he is taxed on a lesser sum than he actually earned. Or he can even show a loss and therefore pay no income tax, and carry over to next year's tax return the amount of loss that brought him beyond zero.

Legitimate uses of the concept of depreciation are possible. If a building were depreciated in, let us say, 40 years, and the landlord received back the cost of the building (his investment)

*Actually much more. See fuller discussion in subsequent pages.

through either income-tax allowances or some other way, it is only logical to require him to declare the building is now at zero cost, and reduce rents to each tenant's proportion of operating and maintenance expenses and taxes.

It must be remembered that in all the 40 years of depreciation referred to, the landlord has made profits from the operations of the building and, having had his entire investment returned to him, he no longer has a legitimate claim to ownership. Of course, if after the 40 years he wished to remain "on staff," so to speak, to manage the building, he would be entitled to the salary of a trained and experienced person.

A lesser variation of the theory of the removal of ownership after depreciation to zero would be to compel a landlord, after full depreciation has been achieved, to construct a new building, of at least the same size and quality. Why not? He has been given back his full investment!

While in this case lower rents, as previously described, would be absent, at least there would be more housing—a not inconsiderable factor for the current housing-starved population. This, too, would remove the pressure of ever higher rents for decaying apartments created by the almost absolute halting of the construction of low- and moderate-income housing. It would also serve the refreshing purpose of the continued renewal of our housing stock, so that our cities would constantly be revived and the inner-city blight that is such an indictment of our form of landlordism would be diminished, if not entirely removed.

Many other variations are possible, but it is not necessary here to develop them. Our point is that no legitimate use is made of depreciation in real estate. Rather, it is a serious though legal abuse and serves only to furnish such huge tax shelters to landlords that they have little interest in providing decent housing for people. They use housing as a means of making more money faster than in most other fields of investment.

The actual fact is that real estate "appreciates," that every building, from a one-family house to a skyscraper office building, sells in each turnover for more than the original cost or the latest purchase price. This, too, removes *any* justification for the use of depreciation as an income-tax deductible expense.

But depreciation is even more complex and more woven through with tax sheltering exceptions than the above discussion would indicate.

For example:

• If the landlord sells a building after a few years of ownership, the new landlord starts all over again and depreciates the building at his new cost, even though it is higher than the original cost.

• If this is done 20 times, with a building now 100 years old—and sold for more each time than was paid for it—depreciation starts anew with each new owner.

• Depreciation on old buildings starts at the rate of 125% of the new cost of the building, not 100%. Don't ask why. It has just been manipulated that way.

• On new residential buildings depreciation is at the rate of 200% of the cost of the building—not 100%.

• Or the landlord can use an even faster method, called "Sum-of-the-Digits," that defies logical relationship to real estate economics—except that it makes more money more quickly for the landlord.

But indignant though you may be at these abuses of the concept of depreciation, they are by no means the worst.

Consider the following: Depreciation is supposed to return to the owner his original capital investment over the useful life of the building. But he gets it not only in the unjustifiable form indicated above; he gets it *twice*: the first time, from the tenants' rents; the second time, from the government in his income tax deduction of depreciation.

Actually, if a landlord is a New York City resident, he gets his depreciation from four sources. The first source is rent from the tenant; the second comes from his federal income tax; the third from his New York State income tax; the fourth from his New York City income tax.

We are content to call it twice—a serious enough commentary—because many states do not have income taxes and very few cities do. Note that (page 15) under the MBR formula, Component 5 (Return on Capital Value, line b, Amortization of

Mortgage, Repayment of Principal), the tenants' rents are based on this repayment of the mortgage principal. The effect is that the tenants buy the building twice over while the landlord continues to own it and reap its continued profits. Land is not depreciable. Therefore, our examples are only approximate and refer to the building only. They are intended to show the nature of real estate/banking and government in the vast and legal conspiracy against tenants.

The depreciation racket seems endless. Since the government knows that landlords do nothing without enticement, a new and even more outrageous form of depreciation called "accelerated depreciation" was enacted.

ACCELERATED DEPRECIATION–AN EXAMPLE:

A special allowance under the income tax laws is given to encourage the rehabilitation of old buildings. The depreciation is at the rate of 100%, but the time allowed for depreciation in rehabilitation is five years, rather than the usual (in an old building) 20 or 30 or so years. The landlords get an incredible bonanza and the tenants get rent increases they cannot afford to pay— sometimes 200% to 300% of the previous rents.

In order to prevent a landlord who rehabilitates a building from taking the five-year depreciation bonanza and then selling it, the law governing this activity requires that he continue to maintain his ownership for a number of years or, as a penalty, the government recaptures appropriate percentages of the bonanza. There is, of course, a loophole large enough to drive a double-decker bus through.

That loophole is that the landlord can avoid the "recapture" of his profits, even if he sells after his five-year depreciation is used up and the building therefore no longer has ultra-fast profit usefulness to him, by the simple device of investing specified percentages of his profits in another rehabilitation.

The legal penalty, therefore, is to "force" the landlord into a larger rehabilitation profit-spree or into two or three smaller ones.

Tables 6 and 7 show Accelerated Depreciation and its effects on a landlord's income tax.

Table 6   *Accelerated Depreciation*

1. The *rehabilitation* costs		$ 1,000,000
The landlord invests 10% or	$100,000	
The mortgage is	900,000	
2. $1,000,000 is depreciated over 5 years.		
Therefore, the depreciation per year is		$ 200,000

The yearly depreciation alone equals 200% of his total cash investment. (Note: For the moment let us disregard such "unimportant" matters as profit from rent, operations, etc.)

The following Table 7 shows an example of the amount and nature of the tax avoidance due to accelerated depreciation.

Table 7   *Effect of Accelerated Depreciation on landlord's income tax*

1. Cash profit from building operations
   (before depreciation allowance) $ 25,000

2. Depreciation (see table 6, item 2)   200,000

3. Net "loss" after depreciation allowance
   (subtract line 2 from line 1)   ($175,000)

4. Suppose the landlord has other income
   from such sources as stocks, bonds,
   interest, salary that he pays himself, of   190,000

5. Therefore, his taxable income is
   (subtract line 3 from line 4)   15,000

6. This amount is taxable on his federal
   income tax at a 25% rate, so his
   income tax is   3,750

Now let us see what would happen without this phony depreciation.

7. Income from dividends, salary, and
   so forth (line 4)   190,000

8. Profits from building before depreciation
   allowance (line 1)   25,000

9. Actual income that *should* be taxable
   (add line 7 and line 8)   215,000

Table 7 (continued)

10. This amount is taxable at a 70% rate,
    so his income tax should be   150,500

11. Thus the landlord should be paying
    $150,500 (line 10) in income tax but,
    thanks to depreciation, he pays only
    $3,750 (line 6), thereby *avoiding*
    federal income taxes in the amount of $146,750

    This amount we taxpayers, who do pay
    our taxes, will have to pay because
    the landlord didn't. This same tax
    avoidance is applicable to state and
    city income taxes.

To summarize:

- It is not required that depreciation allowances be used to construct a new building to replace the aged one.
- Landlords are not even required to repair or refurbish the aging building.
- When depreciation is completed, that is, when the original investment is returned, the rents do not reflect this vital change. Rents, in fact, continue at their old rate or, more probably, rise.
- Depreciation is allowed for shorter periods than the real useful and profitable life of the building.
- In rehabilitation, a five-year depreciation is permitted, which makes for huge tax avoidance and, therefore, profits.
- A building erected 100 years ago for $100,000 which has been sold and resold 20 or so times, each time (up to a certain point) at a profit, is depreciated each time at the rate of 125% of the new, higher purchase price, so that the total amount depreciated may well come to several million dollars over this period.
- Finally, the landlord depreciates his building *twice* over— once in income tax allowance and the second time in the rents he collects.

One may ask how much this racket-type of business contributes to the moral as well as the physical decay of our society.

Abandonment

Abandonment is real estate's most effective propaganda argument.

And why wouldn't the average, ordinary, decent and honest person believe what seems to be a fact of life?

Not being a manipulator or speculator, he or she understands the simple truth that if a commodity is good (profitable), one doesn't throw it away (abandon it). Hence, if one does throw it away (abandon it), it must be no good (unprofitable).

No less an authority than Edward Sulzburger, one of New York's biggest landlords and president of one of New York's major landlord organizations, stated (*New York Times*, November 30, 1975) that 35,000 housing units are being lost each year due to abandonment.

This is a damning fact, a tragedy to each of the 35,000 families forced to look for a new apartment that it hopes to afford in a housing-starved city. Even more tragic is trying to live in an abandoned building, as numberless thousands do, especially but not exclusively in the ghettos.

Abandonment that forces people to live in decay, with no heat in winter; no hot water; frozen pipes that burst and pour water onto floors, walls, and furniture; which in turn cause ceilings to fall, walls to become plasterless, with the exposed lathing becoming the "wall" between one room or one apartment and the next—abandonment is, and should be considered, a crime equal to murder. For, indeed, it has caused the death of innumerable persons—especially infants and children, the aged, the ill and the infirm. It results in fires from building defects, electrical shorts, etc. that kill thousands each year (see your local newspaper).

Abandonment is not a new phenomenon. The 19th century exposés by Jacob Riis depict the horrendous housing conditions of the immigrant ghettos, where whole families were packed into one room; where single people were stacked two or three tiers high, 10 and 15 to a room. No amenities, of course. No painting, plastering, or repairs. The rents were raked in and kept as profits—as near 100% as possible—with expenditures cut well to the bone. If the building collapsed—and they did, and still do (remember the Broadway Central Hotel?)—then the landlord would start with another semidecayed wreck, until perhaps that one went up in flames. Insurance, of course, would help assuage much grief.

So abandonment is not new. It was not invented by the current crop of slumlords. They are just hungry copycats, feeding off the rest of the population in whatever way yields the greatest amount of profit in the shortest amount of time.

THE ECONOMICS OF ABANDONMENT

Yet the landlords tell us that it is *our* fault; that *we* don't pay *them* enough rent to keep *their* properties in good condition! Real estate/banking's major argument is that abandonment is caused by controls on rents. That this is a big lie is clear to many people and certainly to most organized tenants. But knowing that abandonment is tremendously profitable is not enough. We must understand the economics of abandonment. We must know why it is more profitable to abandon a building then to repair, maintain and keep it as a usable, profitable, rentable building.

Abandonment is not a single act, but a process. It starts slowly, takes on more momentum and speeds up toward the end at a breakneck pace. It takes a considerable number of years. Also, *not all* buildings are abandoned—only certain types of buildings.

New buildings, up to 20 years old, are still capable of bringing in top rentals in their various categories. There is much profit to be made, not only from rentals but also from depreciation, capital gains through sales and numerous other devices that abound in this fertile field. So the new building is cared for and maintained as long as it remains in this competitive capacity. After about 20 years, the building gets tired and needs repairs or replacements that may be costly. There has already been depreciation, in addition to operations and maintenance charges that are part of the rent and that are supposed to allow for replacement, so these are not money out of the landlord's pocket.

Now comes the first fateful decision. If it is a Park Avenue or other silk-stocking area building, the probable decision will be to make the necessary investment and, of course, jack up the rent. But if it is a neighborhood into which minorities, especially Black or Latin people, are moving, the probable decision will be to make patchwork or cosmetic repairs. In real estate practice, minority people especially can always be forced to pay more for the same accommodation than white, middle- or upper-income people, and so the landlord can get higher rents without costly replacements.

So here we have the first step in abandonment.

Having taken this step and set his course on this policy, the landlord now decides to get as much money out of the building as possible. This means two things: one, raise the rents to the limit; two, put back into the building as little money as possible.

The difference between the two items is superprofits. This pace, continued another five or ten years, makes for large profits and a building that begins to fall into the category of "shabby or run-down."

Most likely, the building has changed hands a number of times through the years. In the example in Table 2, the landlord amortized in two years $85,500 of his mortgage. Landlords don't like money to lie fallow in a reduced mortgage. The landlord would prefer that money to be in his hands to use as leverage in buying another building. So, in addition to selling at a higher price, he also gains possession of the amortization money.

Thus, turnover in real estate is almost a must!

The new landlord raises the rent because he paid more for the building (see Table 2). By this time, there is not much to be gained by investing money in repairs and upkeep since the building is already shabby. In another number of years and turnover of landlords, the building degenerates from shabby to deteriorated and, finally, to dilapidated. And from there it is only a matter of a few more years to abandonment.

But each of these steps is profitable!

Since we have the percentages and economic facts supplied to us by the good government of the City of New York in the MBR formula, in Table 4, we will apply these, using our $1,000,000 building as a case in point, to see in concrete terms how profitable abandonment is.

The key figure here is 39%, the part of the MBR formula allowed for "Operations and Maintenance Expense." We will omit the very important 7½% annual increase under MBR and the larger increases under "Rent Stabilization." Even though these increase the rents and profits considerably, they would complicate our example, and we want to keep it simple. Therefore, we are making our case by deliberately understating it.

Table 8   *Superprofits from the abandonment process*

1.	Annual rent roll	$150,000
2.	Operations and Maintenance expense (39% x line 1)	$58,000
	After the fateful first step toward abandonment, let us say the landlord reduces his staff, cutting down his Operations and Maintenance expense by "only" 10%.	
3.	This adds to his profit an additional annual amount of	5,850
4.	And let us assume that in four years he sells to another landlord. Total superprofits to date (line 3 x 4 years)	23,400
	Note: In doing these calculations it is necessary to remember two things: one, that this is not the total profit from the building, but only the super-profits based on the *deliberately caused* deterioration; and two, that the total cash investment in the building was only $100,000.	
	The new landlord cuts another 15% of Operations and Maintenance which, when added to the previous landlord's 10% cut, creates a 25% cut in the Operations and Maintenance expense.	
5.	Annual superprofits created by this 25% cut	14,625
6.	If he does this for six years, his superprofits for this period become (line 5 x 6 years)	87,750

(Continued on next page)

7. Total superprofits for ten years
    (line 4 plus line 6)   111,150

    The building is now in the shabby
    class and is sold again. The pace quickens.
    Without detailing each likely step,
    the new slumlord-type landlord makes
    further cuts, taking out another 25%. So,
    the original Operations and Maintenance
    expense has been cut by a total of 50%.

8. Annual superprofits created by 50% cut
    in Operations and Maintenance expense $29,250

9. Superprofits for ten more years, probably
    including more than one landlord
    (line 8 x 10 years)   292,500

10. Total superprofits for the first 20 years
    (line 7 plus line 9)   403,650

    The building is now substantially
    deteriorated and ready for the final
    stages of abandonment. The current
    landlord has bought the building at a lower
    price and is getting all he can as quickly
    as possible. He cuts another 25% of
    Operations and Maintenance for three
    years, so now the original Operations
    and Maintenance expense has been cut by 75%.

11. Annual superprofits created by 75% cut
    in Operations and Maintenance expense   43,875

12. Superprofits for those three years
    (line 11 x 3 years)   131,625

    Now the landlord is ready to go "whole hog"
    and prepares for full abandonment. He
    stops paying real estate taxes, water
    and sewer charges, which are 17.6% of
    the rent roll.

13. Annual superprofits from failure to pay
    real estate taxes, water and sewer charges
    (17.6% x $150,000 rent roll)   26,400

14. It is three* years before the city can
    start in rem or foreclosure proceedings.
    More superprofits (line 13 x 3 years)   79,200

*Note: As of October 7, 1976, Mayor Beame signed into law a bill permit-
ting the city to foreclose in one year rather than three. We will nevertheless

retain the three-year figure, because the city almost never starts in rem proceedings promptly, and the process through the courts is lengthy.

15. The landlord cuts Operations and
    Maintenance another 15% (total cuts are
    now 90% by stopping payment to Con
    Edison and cutting back on fuel.
    (Line 1 x 90%) $52,650

16. Still more superprofits (line 15 x 2 years) $105,300
    The landlord stops paying principal
    on the mortgage for two years.

17. Superprofits from failure to pay mortgage
    principal (45,000 x 2 years)   90,000

    He stops paying interest on the mortgage
    (let us say it has reduced itself to
    $65,000 per year) for two years.

18. Superprofits from failure to pay mortgage
    interest (65,000 x 2 years)   130,000

    Then the landlord cuts out *all* fuel and
    all maintenance (100% of the original
    Operations and Maintenance).

19. Superprofits from elimination of *all*
    Operations and Maintenance for one year   58,500

20. Superprofits for these last six years   594,625

    (Note: Lines 13 to 19 represent
    overlapping, not consecutive, years)

21. Total superprofits (in addition to
    regular profits) in 26 years from point
    of decision not to make necessary
    repairs (line 20 plus line 10) $998,275

    The building is now 45 years old.
    Again, bear in mind that cash investment
    was only $100,000. As the regular
    and superprofits are taken out, as well
    as the capital profits from turnover
    realized, they are usually invested as
    leveraging in additional buildings. Thus
    a new empire is built or an old one expanded.

The many figures contained in the table on abandonment are a weight that we hesitated to impose on the reader. But how else does one expose the enormity of both the amount of money landlords make and the social crimes they commit in the process? How else do we overcome the mass of landlord propaganda with which we have been smothered for years—to the point where the mere utterance of the word "abandonment" is sufficient to "prove" landlord poverty? How else can we arm tenants (and others duped by the real estate/banking industry) so that they join together meaningfully to conduct a struggle for their rights?

Perhaps a lengthy table is not too much burden to bear.

Arson for Profit

There is a logic—perverted to be sure—but a logic, nevertheless, that moves some landlords from the crime against humanity called abandonment to the next criminal step—arson. Are they not tied together by the need to make a profit out of a property? Is not the common denominator of both these acts the profit to be had through the ruination of housing? Is not the premise of this common denominator the cold, cynical, sometimes hateful contempt for the lives, to say nothing of the needs, of people? How can one condemn infants, the ill and the aged, and also the vigorous youth and normally healthy middle-aged people to a winter of no heat and no hot water, for example, unless he has already lost all vestiges of humanity?

If abandonment is profit by slow destruction—and if the abandoned building is still able to yield yet another profit—does it not follow that an attempt should be made to retrieve that profit?

True! Still one has to be extra careful. While many laws, the housing code included, have broken down to the point where a landlord can violate them with impunity, the fact is that the laws against arson have not yet so completely degenerated. They are merely in the process of breaking down.

And again, there are so many things that can go wrong. One can even get caught! And if a high wind should spread the flames too far and people get burned to death, then there can be an awful cry for a real investigation. This can be very uncomfortable. So one must be cautious.

Try not to do it yourself. Get someone else to do it for you. Or, best of all, get some of the slum kids who have already been deformed by slum existence. You can get them more cheaply than a grown-up and, best of all, if the kids are caught, they don't go to jail but to Children's Court. This rickety piece of the machinery of justice is so bogged down in corruption, understaffing and cynicism, that it makes little attempt at the rehabilitation of youth, but becomes a revolving door. In and out they go, until they are old enough to go to jail, which then becomes a postgraduate course in crime.

Jack Newfield and Paul DuBrul, in their book *The Abuse of Power*, say that in the Borough of the Bronx in one year, 1975, in just a 12-square-mile area in its southern part, there were 13,000 fires! Forty people were killed. They then go on to quote District Attorney Mario Merola as believing that most of the torching is instigated by landlords to collect fire insurance.

That arson for profit is not a figment of the fevered imaginations of those who have an anti-landlord bias is proven by the organ of the landlords themselves, the *Real Estate Weekly*. In its issue of February 16, 1976, it states: "Landlords set fire to unrentable or unmanageable buildings to salvage at least their insurance." Further along in the same article it hopes that the mass exodus of people from this area caused by arson and the policy of "planned shrinkage"—that is, the withholding of all services necessary to make it livable—will result in its conversion to an industrial park. At a profit, of course!

Reuben Klein, President of the New York Realty Owners Association and the Bronx Realty Advisory Board, in the *New York Post* of April 27, 1977, tried to shift the blame from landlords who torch their own properties for insurance, onto—of course—that evil of all evils, rent control. He then says, "There may well be instances in which owners in desperation have had their own buildings set on fire." We are talking here about a growing phenomenon, the logic of which is inherent in our for-profit private landlordism.

A few quotes from the press should suffice to underscore the point.

> Edward Richburg and his 21-year-old son Edward Jr. were arrested trying to torch their building in the Bronx. They offered the arresting detective $137 cash and more later, to forget the charges.
>
> *(New York Times,* June 6, 1975)

> 8 landlords and associates were indicted in Bronx fires.
>
> *(New York Times,* June 12, 1975)

> A *New York Times* headline, June 23, 1977, says, "Arson for Profit Reported on Rise, with Cost of $2 Billion Last Year."

> Again, June 16, 1977, another *New York Times* headline exclaims that "Serious Fires in New York City have jumped 40% in last 3 years."

> And, finally, August 4, 1977, the *New York Post* headlines the fact: "26 suspicious fires reported in one day," and goes on to explain that this is "triple the daily average."

Tax shelters (and handouts from the public treasury)

Tax shelters are what distinguish the wealthy and the vastly wealthy from the plain people, who, essentially, carry the burden of the cost of government on their backs.

The relationship between profit and income taxes is too clear to need much elaboration. As Alan S. Oser stated in his *New York Times* column, "About Real Estate" (March 9, 1976), "By writing off the mortgage interest and real estate taxes during the construction period, and by taking accelerated depreciation on the asset, *the investor might hope to realize anywhere from $3 to $5 of tax losses on each $1 invested."* (Emphasis added)

We have seen from our study of accelerated depreciation how that tax shelter resulted in a tax avoidance of $146,750. This represented $1.50 of tax avoidance for each $1.00 that the landlord invested, which according to Oser is a third of the amount a sophisticated investor would hope to realize.

There exists an enormous body of law granting tax exemptions and tax shelters. These are further enlarged by judicial interpretations and Internal Revenue Service regulations. To get full information on all the tax rip-offs, it would be necessary to subscribe to a law library service or any of the weighty volumes of the publishers of the tax services.

We have undertaken, instead, to discuss in some detail two specific tax-shelter giveaways. The first is a study of the "shrinking tax base." It should be useful in removing at least one layer of the shroud that surrounds us and prevents us from observing how often and how extensively we are being robbed by those we elect to serve our interests. The second is a classic study of the subsidized housing rip-off—using New York's Mitchell-Lama Law as our example.

But before we do, it seems only proper to give a skeleton indication of how far, wide and deeply ingrained into our society is this Robin Hood-in-reverse syndrome.

So here follow a few, but only a sprinkling, of the many tax-sheltering devices that make our rich economy so rich for the rich and so devastatingly poor for the poor.

• *Property taxes*—Paid by the tenant as part of rent, but income tax deductible by the landlord.

• *Real Estate Investment Trust (REIT)*—A form of organization that allows investors to pool their money for large-scale real estate investment. Then, as long as the REIT distributes, in the form of dividends to the investors, 90% of its taxable income, no corporate taxes need be paid on that income.

Investment in REITs was built into an enormous inverted pyramid so fragile that it has now almost totally collapsed, causing the loss of hundreds of millions of dollars to REIT owners and sponsors, including many major banks, and causing deep concern among bank supervisory agencies.

• *Syndications*—A legal device whereby the general or managing partner sells shares of the profits and a proportion of the amount of tax-sheltering depreciation to limited partners, who, to make the investment practical, must have high incomes. The limited partner pays to the general partner a portion of the invested capital and receives in return a share of the profits. What is more important—in fact, the essence of the deal—is that the limited partner receives the right to his proportion of the amount of depreciation allowance. The limited partner deducts the depreciation allowance, which the law allows him to show as a loss, from his other income, thereby showing a net income smaller than the actual one.

Example:

Income from other sources	$100,000
Depreciation tax shelter (proportion)	−30,000
Taxable income	$ 70,000

• *Lease-backs*

There are numerous devices which, through the use of lease-back hocus-pocus, reduce or avoid taxes. The essence of this device is to construct a building, sell it to another owner, who in turn provides a long-term lease at specified rents to the original builder/occupant.

The new owner gets his profits and depreciation, etc. But the builder/occupant, who assumes all maintenance and other costs, instead of being able to depreciate only 2½% per year (over 40 years), is able to charge off the entire annual rental as well as maintenence costs, etc. as expenses—thus providing the basis for far greater tax deductions.

There are many angles to lease-backs, but a substantial part lies in the fact that land costs cannot be depreciated by the owner. However, when land costs are part of rental payments, they are permitted to be charged off as an expense.

The variants of this device are many, but one is worthy of repetition. Gerald J. Robinson, the author of *Federal Taxation of*

Real Estate, cites, under the heading of Financing Techniques, the glories of:

 • *The Bondable Net Lease.* He describes it thus:

"To the real estate investor, paradise is a place where all cash flow is sheltered, paper losses are generated for tax purposes, and the purchase can be 'mortgaged out'—that is —100% of the cost can be financed so that the investor need not put up any of his own money."

He then goes on to explain the details of the operation and the amount of profit to be made thereby, and concludes that the return is "infinite"—that is, immeasurable, since there was no investment on which to calculate a percentage of profit.

 • *The Inflated Mortgage*—The seller with an angle who, having come close to the completion of a deal, decides that for him a capital gain is most desirable, persuades the buyer to increase the amount of the purchase price, as well as the mortgage, by a specific amount and reduce the rate of interest by a compensating amount—so that the number of dollars paid over the period of the mortgage is identical. Presto! The seller gets a capital gain taxable at half the rate of the income he would have had to pay as the recipient of the mortgage interest payments.

 • *The Deflated Mortgage*—The reverse of the above. A lower sales price, a smaller mortgage, but a higher interest rate, are arranged so that over the period of the length of the mortgage, the number of dollars exchanged is identical. In this case, the buyer wants large interest payments, because he can charge this off to Uncle Sam as an income tax deduction.

This can go on until we reach the four-inch thickness of the tomes that advise our speculators on how better to speculate. But the examples furnished herein should serve as indicators of the ingenuity applied to the dual process of extracting the maximum from the tenant and paying the minimum (or perhaps nothing) to the government in taxes.

The history of government-
subsidized housing programs

It is important to note that every scheme introduced that
supposedly would provide new housing for those who needed it,
at rents they could afford, was actually designed to make great
profits for the banks, developers and builders, while only inciden-
tally providing housing for a small percentage of the population.

Stuyvesant Town, sponsored by Metropolitan Life Insurance Company, was built with bonds floated under the provisions
of the New York State Urban Redevelopment Act, in 1943. Even
then, more than 30 years ago, only 3% of those living in the area
could afford to pay the rents. Metropolitan Life was not forced to
relocate those who had lived for years in the ramshackle tene-
ments that were replaced. Moreover, it was only after a monu-
mental and pioneering campaign that Metropolitan Life was
forced to accept the tenancy of even one Black couple.

The Slum Clearance Program enacted as part of the 1937
Federal Housing Act was the beginning of a plan to clear the
slums. It was not to build new, decent and affordable housing for
the residents of these areas, nor to beautify the city, but to tear
down the old housing and pave the way for higher realty values.

The carrot for the investor/speculator was provided by the
condemnation of land through the city's exercise of eminent
domain. It was not just condemned, of course, but also given to
the builder/speculator at only a small fraction of the cost of the
land. The difference between this "knock-down" price and the
actual cost was made up by the federal government and the
city—in other words, the taxpayers.

This profitable process was repeated in many cities. Man-
hatttanville and Lincoln Center are but two examples in New
York City.

The Housing Act of 1949 substituted the phrase "Title I" for
the phrase "Slum Clearance Program" in the 1937 Act, which by
then had fallen into disrepute. Some low-rent housing was built,
but under the Title I cover, there was also built the New York
Coliseum—by no stretch of the most fertile imagination low-rent
housing.

In order to get away from the massive slum-clearance program, the 1954 Housing Act initiated the provision of subsidies to banks and developers, under programs set forth in Sections 221(d) (3), 221(d) (6), and 236, among others. In every instance, when a loan was given to a developer at the interest rate of 1% or 3%, in the early days of those programs, lower rents per room resulted. Where 1% interest was charged, the rents per room per month dropped by $40 to $50 below comparable apartments. The difference between the 1% paid by the developer to the bank and the market interest rate was paid to the bank by HUD out of our taxes so that the banks, as usual, got the full market rate.

But shortly thereafter, the rents would begin to rise toward the same market levels as the noninterest subsidized buildings, since the drive of a builder or speculator is not for low rents but for maximum profits.

The 1974 Housing and Community Development Act, one of the first laws signed by the non-elected President Ford, spelled out a new subsidy program called Section 8, which is in current use.

SECTION 8

Supposedly designed to benefit low-income tenants, Section 8 in fact serves only to swell the landlords' coffers. According to the legislation, owners rent new or existing housing units directly to low-income tenants who are certified for the program. A tenant pays 15% to 25% of his or her income for rent; the difference between that amount and the contract rent is made up by a HUD Housing Assistance Payment to the landlord.

HUD establishes the Section 8 contract rent ceilings and adjusts (read, raises) them annually. The net effect of these ceilings is that new and higher rental standards are set throughout the area. In the New York metropolitan area, for example, the Section 8 ceiling rent for a new two-bedroom apartment in an elevator building is $684 per month; the ceiling for a two-bedroom apartment in an existing building is $266 per month, but rent-controlled or rent-stabilized apartments renting under Section 8 are automatically decontrolled, guaranteeing that rents will continue to soar.

To utilize Section 8 subsidies, owners of new housing must first seek HUD approval of their proposed units, while owners of existing housing must be sought out by the tenants themselves. However, many landlords of existing housing refuse to make Section 8 agreements. Apparently they dislike the administrative hassles but, more importantly, they fear the inspection of their properties that is required before HUD approves the agreements. While thousands of tenants are certified under Section 8, only a small fraction of those qualified have been able to take advantage of the Section 8 program, because of this landlord reluctance. Tenants are forced to compete with each other for the few units that are available under Section 8 and to pay higher rents for non-Section 8 units.

Because Section 8 rent standards succeed in boosting rents in contiguous areas and buildings, and since the housing shortage not only persists but is aggravated as time goes by, more landlords are refusing to accept Section 8 tenants. They reason that if they can get the high Section 8 rents without the Section 8 requirements of acceptable standards of maintenance, the same amount of rent will yield even more profits.

THE NEW YORK STATE URBAN
DEVELOPMENT CORPORATION

It is difficult, in the vast welter of examples from which to make minimal choices, to omit citing—if ever so incompletely— the Rockefeller gift to humanity known as the Urban Development Corporation (UDC).

Financed with New York State funds and an almost open-ended borrowing capacity in the form of the authority to issue tax-exempt bonds, the UDC was empowered to go almost anywhere and do almost anything—even superseding city and county laws, restrictions, regulations and building codes.

It cut a wide swath, built high-cost housing, Roosevelt Island among them, and spent money like the proverbial drunkard. Result: It was saved from bankruptcy only by an emergency direct appropriation from the New York State Legislature of $200 million and a "loan" of an additional $258.

THE NEW YORK CITY
MUNICIPAL LOAN PROGRAM

Ostensibly created to aid in the rehabilitation of structurally sound housing, it is a corrupt piece of cynicism that brings rents up 100% or more and out of reach of the existing tenants, while the landlord reaps rich rewards by doing shabby cosmetic and often fraudulent work. Mayor Lindsay was forced to close down the program for about six months because the smell of the scandals was too much for even his insensitive nose! Defaults have reached almost 70%. The program no longer functions, but landlords who "rehabbed" housing with the fund continue to get rent increases.

These are but samples of the duplicity, cynicism and waste of billions of dollars—each of which, in its turn, has become a costly and vast failure, that provides no solution to the housing problem.

The "shrinking tax base" and the massive real estate giveaway

The City of New York has built up a mountainous debt—now about $13 billion. While it cannot be said that none of it has resulted in usefulness to its citizens, the fact is that an unknown but considerable portion of the debt has gone off into sidetracks, ranging from the outright thievery of Boss Tweed and his many past and current successors to the inflated costs of many projects completed and under construction. An example of the former is the $2 billion actually appropriated in the 1920's for the building of the Second Avenue subway; the money disappeared and there is no subway, nor was there ever a serious investigation. An example of the latter is the Yankee Stadium rehabilitation, budgeted at $24 million, which ended costing about $100 million.

The costs of running the city, both actually needed and profligately wasted, have resulted in ever mounting taxes. The greatest bulk of taxation shifts yearly away from corporations and wealthy individuals onto the shoulders of the citizenry—not equally, of course, but resting most heavily on the poor, in proportion to the degree of their poverty.

The wounded cries that arise from our city officials when needed improvements in facilities or services are demanded, are enough to make the naive believe that not another dollar can be raised from any possible source. During the course of the city's fiscal crisis of the 70's, the whipping boy has been the "shrinking tax base."

This was the excuse, for example, for denying for about two years the same limited rent-increase relief to the very elderly poor in Mitchell-Lama housing as the city had extended to the same elderly poor in privately owned housing. At the same time, while it denied a paltry few millions of dollars to these elderly poor, the city administration handed out many hundreds of millions to real estate/banking and others who are well-heeled and politically useful. In subsequent pages there will be found few examples of the huge assessment reductions to the largest and most powerful corporations in New York City—adding up to many tens of millions of dollars.

Many interesting facts are contained in a report dated May 20, 1977, called Official Statement [Relating to the Issuance of] $500,000,000 City of New York General Obligation Serial Bonds. Such reports, with their revealing and candid contents, are necessary in connection with bond issues. Bankers, bond houses and large buyers do not deal in myths. They are hardheaded and want the facts unvarnished; otherwise they will not lend money or buy bonds. So the city perforce states the truth, for a change. But this truth does not reach the public, does not get printed in the daily press. Such statements or prospectuses are carefully distributed and are intended to reach the hands of the elite of bankers and other buyers of bonds in large quantities.

A few selected facts from the Official Statement will illuminate our subject.

The assessed valuation of taxable real estate in New York City was $38.065 billion in 1973. In 1977, it reached $39.025 billion, an increase of slightly under $1 billion in five years of substantial new construction, rising real estate values and especially rising rents.

As an example, let us take the sector of housing that is most "restricted" in its ability to increase rents—rent-controlled housing. Under the MBR law, rent is increased 7½% per year, compounded, of course. Therefore, in this least desirable sector of housing (from the landlord's point of view) in the five years 1973-1977, rents rose by 54.3% as a result of the MBR law and including 1977's labor cost passalong—without taking into account the other methods of obtaining rent increases, such as hardship, major capital improvements, new stoves, refrigerators, screens, etc.

The increases in profits, and therefore the market values of the buildings, are nowhere reflected in the assessed valuations of the properties.

Another example of this is the famed Rockefeller Center, as mean a landlord as any other. Commercial rents in these buildings have been rising regularly and substantially with each lease renewal. A few years ago the Rockefeller management, instead of getting a plain, ordinary rent increase, decided to increase the square footage (this is the basis of rent calculations in commercial real estate) by the simple device of measuring the occupied area to the *outside wall* of the building and to the *center line of the common corridor.*

Let us illustrate the effect on an occupant of a small office 30 ft. x 20 ft., with the 30 feet along the outside wall and corridor, and the 20 feet adjoining other offices and therefore separated by only thinner interior walls, which the Rockefellers generously do not count. This space was, when rented, 600 square feet. But with 18-inch walls and one-half of the 10-foot corridors, another 130 square feet are added, so that the 600 square feet suddenly stretch to 730. It does not matter that these 130 square feet are not useable space. They are now paid for at the same rate as the other 600 square feet. This 21½% rent increase is not reflected in the assessed valuation of Rockefeller Center. In fact, it is more likely that the Rockefeller Center management will petition for a decrease in assessed valuation.

Back again to the city's assessed valuation. This same table has in its next column the figures on *"Full valuation."* In 1973, the figure was $69.209 billion and in 1977 it jumped to $81.303 billion, a rise in those five years of $12.09 billion.

So the *assessed valuation* rose at the rate of about 1/12 that of the *full valuation*. It is clear beyond all doubt that the city itself has been shrinking the tax base for the benefit of the real estate industry, while pretending that this shrinkage was inescapably related to the city's crises—and therefore must be paid for by decreases in city services.

Even worse, the propaganda that emanates from both real estate/banking and the government blames the shrinkage on abandoned buildings, which, in turn, they blame on rent controls. (See page 24, the section on the causes and profitability of abandonment.) The "shrinking tax base" lament is as pernicious as it is hypocritical. The city has an unvarying policy of constant giving to real estate and big business and diminishing every important service required by the people.

As stated earlier, the giant corporations are granted assessed valuation reductions each year. In 1977, the real estate tax rate was *reduced* by five cents per $100 of assessed valuation—this in the face of a "shrinking tax base." The Mayor has promised a reduction in stock transfer taxes and their virtual elimination in not too many years. He likewise has promised sharp decreases in commercial rent taxes and in other levies on business, industry and finance.

A press release dated May 24, 1977, issued by the New York City Planning Commission, offers an almost prostrate city to the American Stock Exchange for its expansion program. The following is a quotation from the press release:

> The city's incentive program contained tax exemptions that would aid in the financing of the new facility—either construction of a new one or renovation of an existing structure.
>
> Also, the city and state are *prepared to arrange financing* for a

new Amex facility *through issuance of revenue bonds by a public benefit corporation* [meaning tax-exempt bonds at a lower interest rate] such as the Urban Development Corporation, assuming sufficient cash flow to support debt coverage.

If the new Amex facility is located on public land, *the city is willing to write down the cost of the land through favorable acquisition or lease terms* with the Amex.

(Comment in brackets and emphasis added)

Like the State of New York, the city's program is designed to "bribe the private sector," as was so inelegantly and bluntly stated by a New York City housing official a few years ago.

LOCAL LAW J-51

In line with the policy—which, reduced to its essence, means: lay off the powerful and mobile rich and soak the locked-in, immobile, unorganized and defenseless poor—the City of New York has enacted a law entitled J-51, which does just that, but with a special vengeance.

This law to encourage rehabilitating commercial buildings and converting old lofts and hotels to residential properties, as well as rehabilitating run-down residential buildings, provides the following incentives:

• A 12-year exemption from an increase in assessed valuation attributable to the "reasonable cost" of the renovation is granted.

• The remainder of the tax on the building and land for nine to 20 years is abated, up to 90% of the reasonable cost of the work, with a limit of 8.5% in any one year.

• If any year's abatement is greater than the tax due, the owner's tax is reduced to zero, with the remaining dollars of abatement available through the 20th year.

None of these rehabilitations and the tax giveaways that are the essence of J-51 result in living quarters for either poor or middle-income people. That is to say, 75% to 85% of New York's population, while shouldering the tax costs of this law, are ineligible to receive its benefits.

A few examples:

Rents in the Chelsea Towers start at $300 per month for studio apartments and go as high as $700 for one-bedroom furnished apartments.

(Our Town, November 12, 1976)

155 East 23 St., a renovated 1890 factory structure, costs $120 per room per month.

(New York Times, December 10, 1976)

244 Madison Ave., a 180-unit building after renovation, rents from $350 per month for a studio to $550 per month for a two-bedroom apartment.

Such examples and some even more disgracefully expensive can be recited at length, but the purposes of the law and its effects become totally clear when we examine some of the responses of the real estate industry.

Martin B. Swarzman, a 45-yeai-old real estate developer, calls J-51 "very enlightened."

(New York Times, May 30, 1976)

Charles Kaiser of the *New York Times* (February 15, 1976) says that J-51 "makes it possible for a builder to recoup approximately 60% of his investment through real estate tax reductions and has sparked investor interest."

Eugene J. Morris, real estate lawyer, says J-51 "is the only game in town."

(Real Estate Weekly, March 22, 1976)

LOCAL LAW 58

The warm embrace that the real estate/banking industry gave to J-51 encouraged the New York City lawmakers to enact a sequel. If we can have in the movies not only "Frankenstein" but "Son of Frankenstein," and "Godfather" followed by "Godfather, Part II," and if "King Kong" is good enough to produce a 1976 version of the 1930's moneymaker, than why not another J-51? So it came to pass.

On November 4, 1976, the Mayor signed Local Law 58 of 1976. While J-51 gave away the city's tax resources for converting old buildings into expensive housing, Local Law 58 creates additional tax-base shrinkage by providing tax incentives for commercial and industrial building, both newly constructed and rehabilitated.

The nature of this Christmas package is:

• *Reconstruction*

The building will receive tax exemption, starting at 95% of the difference between the assessed valuation at the time of the application and the assessed valuation at the completion of construction; the exemption being decreased at the rate of 5% for the subsequent 19 years.

• *New construction*

The tax exemption is for 50% of the same difference as above for a 10-year period, reduced at the rate of 5% each year.

(Campaign contributions can be expected to be substantial this year.)

SECTION 421

Section 421 of the New York State Real Property Tax Law is a statute similar in effect to J-51 and Local Law 58. Landlords who have been enticed to take advantage of Section 421 include the late Aristotle Onassis. Onassis and his partner Arlen Realty applied for a $6,000,000 tax exemption under Section 421 for Olympic Towers, the mixed-use high-rise structure on exclusive, mid-town Fifth Avenue. Olympic Towers includes 15 stories of office space and 30 stories of condominiums—hardly the low- or middle-income housing that Section 421 was designed to encourage.

Thus it becomes clear—and endless more evidence can be adduced—that the "shrinking tax base" is not the result of actions caused by some external force too powerful for the city to cope with. The city is not the victim of the "shrinking tax base"; it is the organizer and the perpetrator of this nefarious device. Worse yet, the city uses the inevitable results to force its citizens into accepting greater poverty, more inconveniences and fewer vital services.

A *detailed and perhaps classic example*
of the workings of subsidized housing

Over the years we have heard the magic names of the varied new laws (mostly federal) that would lead us out of the backwoods of insufficient, deteriorated and too-expensive housing and into the shining new world of clean, bright, modern and affordable places to live.

Thus we have had the Urban Renewal Program, the General Neighborhood Renewal Program, the Neighborhood Development Program, the Model Cities Program, the New Towns Program, and so many others. Note that each name was designed to stir the hopes of the beleaguered rent-payers and led us to believe that if we waited just a little longer the bright future of our fairyland dreams would come true. Yet each of these programs lasted its few years, spent many millions of dollars and then faded away, only to be replaced by another program with an even more hope-provoking name.

The common denominator of all these schemes is not housing for people, but housing as the instrument with which to enrich the banker, builder, speculator, real estate operator, and their associates. Each program resulted in a financial superstructure so large that the costs of maintaining it—that is, paying off the inflated mortgage, the bonds that financed it and the interest charges it had racked up—brought the cost of the minimal amount of housing produced beyond the means of all but upper-income people.

New York State and New York City officials also have played the dual game of giving the people hopes and giving their political contributors something more real and substantial. Thus there was enacted a law called the Mitchell-Lama Law. Since we have at hand a rich amount of detailed insight into its workings, let us examine it with some care, bearing in mind that it is really a prototype for all subsidized housing—give or take a few details and variations.

MITCHELL-LAMA HOUSING

The Mitchell-Lama Law, so named to honor its sponsors in the New York State legislature, is more formally known as the New York State Private Finance Law. Its sponsors just happened to be a lawyer and an architect. It also just happened that State Senator MacNeil Mitchell's law firm did most of the legal work for the early aspiring or successful Mitchell-Lama promoters. The same universal, unwritten law that provided so well for Senator Mitchell also just happened to make Assemblyman Alfred Lama's architectural firm foremost in the design and planning of the early namesake projects.

The law, which calls itself a low-income housing law, defines low income by stating that a family of up to three members may earn an annual income of not more than six times the annual rent charged in such a project, while larger families may earn incomes up to seven times the rent. It then proceeds to place no limit on its rents nor on the income of its occupants. The results are so ludicrous that a family of four in a six-room apartment (with balcony) can earn over $50,000 per year and still be considered low income, and therefore be eligible to have its rents subsidized by the people of the state or the city of New York, including its poorest taxpayers.

This type of law is not a 20th century phenomenon, except in its refinements; its traditions reach back to the founding of our country.

A foremost example is the granting by Congress in the mid-19th century of millions of acres to the railroad barons at trifling cost, with almost no money put up in advance. These beneficiaries then proceeded to market this land nationwide at thousands of percent profit.

In those crude days, it was not uncommon to give stock in the enterprise—free or at nominal cost—to useful dignitaries, run-

ning the gamut from legislators to governors, to members of the
Supreme Court and, if you please, to the Vice President of the
United States and, it has been suggested, even to Presidents.
With such devices the wheels of official approval not only spun
easily, but the public also was assured its investment was secure.

While it cannot be said that similar methods are not employed today, nevertheless the cries of outrage that ensued from
the booms and busts that dot our economic history have made it
necessary to refine the methods used in the extraction of these
huge and often obscene profits, so that they are less visible to the
naked eye.

Rather than burden this document with an example of each
of the 57 varieties of real estate rip-offs, let us select one—a good
one, to be sure—which is more or less a prototype and which
serves its beneficiaries so well.

MANHATTAN PLAZA

In restating some of the essential highlights of this complex
deal, we wish to give credit to its source, Robert Schur, who has in
the past served in New York City as Deputy Administrator of the
Housing and Development Administration and, having lived in
the belly of the beast, knows it well. He has also been the
Executive Director of the Association of Neighborhood Developers and has published the facts in their paper, *City Limits*,
issues of February/March and April 1977.

The action takes place under the protective mantle of the
New York State Mitchell-Lama Law, the benefits of which the
state has likewise extended to the City of New York.

There was assembled a square block of down-at-the-heels
buildings running from Ninth to Tenth Avenues and from 42nd to
43rd Streets in the skid-row area near Times Square in Manhattan. The tenants—residential and storekeepers—were evicted by
methods too well known to need repetition. Until the assemblage
of the properties was ready for higher purposes, it served to stave
off starvation as a parking lot.

The assembler was a well-known real estate entrepreneur,
Seymour Durst, who owned large amounts of other property in

the surrounding, likewise run-down, area. If this square block could be made into a respectable area, the property values of Durst's other holdings would increase immeasurably.

With this in mind, Durst sold this square block to an influential real estate promoter/speculator/builder by the name of Richard Ravitch, president of the nationwide HRH Construction Company, a name to be reckoned with. The terms and conditions of this sale are not known.

Ravitch's influence with those in the New York State hierarchy, whose duty it is to approve Mitchell-Lama applications, was not sufficient to overcome their disbelief that people who could afford $100 per month per room (the projected rent in the late 1960s) would move into such a decrepit and forbidding area. They said no.

But Ravitch's resourcefulness—and especially his political contacts—were not yet at an end. He moved over to the New York City officialdom, where his reception was warmer.

Since the city has the same power as the state in such matters, he put forward his plans for "Manhattan Plaza."

The City underwrites it

The budgeted cost was to be $95 million for the 1968 apartment complex. The city would finance 95% or about $90 million and Ravitch would put up an equity of 5%—or about $5 million. However, the $5 million needn't be put up at once. Only $150,000 was required at the outset. Ravitch could pay the balance later out of the $90 million he collected from the city to construct the building.

It should be noted here that one of the "beauties" of Mitchell-Lama is that the city issues tax-exempt bonds to raise the money to pay for the construction, etc. If Ravitch were to borrow from private banking sources at standard rates, the interest would be approximately double, or if a second mortgage was required, considerably more than double.

Omitting much interesting and even dramatic detail, let us establish the fact that the city was less concerned with the problem of such high rents in such a low neighborhood than was the state, and approved the project.

The profits commence

Precisely one day after the deal was closed and the contract with the city signed, Ravitch sold his equity to a syndicate headed by Estée Lauder of beauty products fame, and her equally famous husband, Alexander Cohen, the theatrical producer. Thus, while the enterprise was still a parking lot, with not a shovelful of earth moved, Ravitch ceased to be the owner-sponsor.

From this syndicate he received the sum of $12 million for the transfer of ownership. Thus he profited $7 million ($12 million less $5 million eventually due as equity) on a cash investment of $150,000!

However, the game is not yet over. While Ravitch ceased to be the owner/sponsor, he still continued to be the builder (or at least his company, the HRH Construction Co., was). The construction contract was worth some $60 million. The builder's overhead and profit are acknolwledged parts of cost. Whether these two items came to 25% or somewhat more or less is for the reader to guess.

In addition, the Mitchell-Lama law provides fees and percentages of costs for all sorts of necessities and goodies, going the range from acquisition of land, cost of demolition, relocation of tenants and interest on money borrowed by the builder to acquire the land and erect the building until completion, all the way to real estate, water and sewer taxes during the construction period, insurance premiums for fire and liability, title insurance, recording fees, real estate transfer tax and fees for filing building plans. Added to all these are allowances for lawyers' fees and expenses. The architects' fee is calculated as a percentage of the cost of construction.

In the case of HRH and other such firms, they have their own "captive" architects and lawyers on retainer, so that these fees in large part remain with HRH and Ravitch.

There are also builders' and developers' fees, which, in a project of this size, Robert Schur estimates to be worth approximately $3 million; and whereas with Ravitch and HRH they are one and the same, they nevertheless collect both parts of the fee. Since the city permits the developer to "return" the "developer's fee" as a credit against equity, the net cash outlay for this purpose becomes—not $5 million—but $2 million (not counting any of the above-listed residual profits).

Here it should be noted that the extras, goodies and emoluments with which the Mitchell-Lama law rewards the worthy sponsors, builders and developers not only enriches them but also helps the impoverishment process of the future tenants. All of these "costs" are added to the mortgage, which, even at moderate interest rates, severely inflate the rents. However, as shall be seen, the interest rates became anything but moderate.

Through all of this divestiture to Estée Lauder and friends, Ravitch, in addition to retaining his lucrative status as builder of the project also continued to be, through another corporation, the managing agent of the complex. The law and its subordinate regulations allow for this purpose 4% per year of the rent roll. The estimated gross rentals were to be over $6 million per year, which gave Ravitch some quarter of a million dollars per year to look forward to.

Why do investors put up such large sums?

At this point the question arises: Why did Estée Lauder and her associates agree to turn over to Ravitch the rather healthy sum of $12 million for a project on which not a hole had been dug nor a brick had been laid? The answer is to be found in what is really the name of the game—that is, the income tax laws and the tax shelters they provide for the rich and the super-rich.

The role of the Income Tax laws in real estate

The income tax laws require unmarried persons to fork over to Uncle Sam 70% of all income over $100,000 per year (for married folk it is $200,000 per year), a rather unpleasant prospect on April 15.

But Uncle Sam taketh away and Uncle Sam giveth to the deserving wealthy. The Internal Revenue Code provides as one of its tax shelters that for newly constructed multiple-dwelling housing, the owner may use a device called depreciation at 200% of cost on declining balances—technically known as double declining balances.

In the Lauder situation it works something like this for the first year:

Manhattan Plaza cost Lauder *et al.* $12 million; the city put up $90 million, making a total of $102 million. The land, which does not depreciate, let us assume cost $7 million. There remains to be depreciated $95 million. The time period specified for such a building is 40 years. Therefore, it depreciates at the rate of 2½% per year, or by $2.375 million each year.

But by using the double declining balance method, the 2½% becomes 5% and the dollar figures turn into $4.75 million during the first year's depreciation. Note Appendix II to see how long it takes for the Lauder syndicate to: a) get its investment back, and b) begin to shelter (that is, pay no income taxes on) their income from other sources.

But here we must take a moment to explain that the Mitchell-Lama law is a limited dividend law and that the owners are not permitted to earn more than 6% per annum on their cash equity. However, this 6% dividend is calculated as part of the rent, and thus is guaranteed to the owners. Applied to Manhattan Plaza, 6% of $5 million is $300,000 per year.

If, then, we subtract $4,750,000 of depreciation "loss" from $300,000 of income, we come up with a "loss" for income tax purposes of $4,450,000. This "loss" is divided, pro rata, among the Lauder partners, and renders totally tax-free all their other income up to the amount of their prorated share.

Schur uses the following example to show its practical effect in the Lauder/Cohen case. Presuming each had a 10% share, the total for both would be 20% and thus they would be eligible for 20% of the depreciation "loss" from Manhattan Plaza, or $890,000 during the first year.

If—and we're just guessing—they had a combined net income from stocks, bonds, interest, salaries, royalties, dividends and what not, of $1,500,000, their tax at 70% would be $1,020,980. But they now have a "depreciation loss" that subtracts $890,000 from their $1,500,000 income. Therefore the taxable income becomes $610,000, and their income tax falls to $397,980—a saving during the first year of $623,000!

This represents a return on their combined investment of

$2.4 million (20% of $12 million) or just about 25% during the first year! Add to this the 20% share of the $300,000 (profit from operations), or $60,000 as the Lauder/Cohen share, and the figure jumps to over 28%.

We have developed a table as Appendix II showing the effects of the double declining balances depreciation allowance and the tax-shelter benefits for the Lauder/Cohen share of the enterprise.

It is worthy of note that the total of tax-shelter savings at the end of 4 years is $2,296,266 for the Lauder/Cohen ménage—just short of their $2.4 million investment. However, to this we must add 4 years at $60,000 cash-flow profit from operations, which brings their total profit to $2,536,266 or $136,266 more than their entire investment.

Yet they continue to own 20% of Manhattan Plaza and get the continuing tax-shelter benefits as well as cash-flow income—in all successive years—without one cent of remaining cash investment.

In the double declining balances racket it is obvious—and this is its point—that the majority of the depreciation comes in the first few years, and the remainder diminishes slowly thereafter. The result is that 50% of the total depreciation comes in the first 13 years, while the remaining 50% is stretched out over the subsequent 27 years in ever diminishing amounts. Thus in not too many years, Lauder/Cohen will have extracted most of their accelerated depreciation from this project and will sell it to another operator/speculator to have him put it to his own special depreciation uses. The new operator/speculator will start depreciation all over again, this time at "only" 125% of whatever it is he will have paid for it (minus, of course, the land value).

In addition to the income-tax angle, and the free ownership after 4 years angle, one should not forget the long-term capital-gains angle. When the depreciation declines to the points where it is no longer superprofitable to them, Lauder/Cohen will sell to another millionaire in need of a tax shelter for however many millions of dollars the then current market will bear. Long-term capital gains are taxed at about one-half of ordinary income.

Here it is important to underscore a quite obvious point,

mostly for the sake of those belonging to the school of thought that considers it fine for people who are that smart to make all their superior brains allow. That foolishness aside, it isn't only the Lauder/Cohen riches that are the problem. The fact is that all the honest (and poorer) taxpayers pick up this burden in their own higher tax payments. The U.S. budget is not decreased by the amount of the Lauder/Cohen tax shelter. It remains the same. The share of the paying taxpayers is necessarily that much higher.

The quick path to riches encounters some trouble

When Robert Burns formulated his well-known phrase about the best-laid plans of mice and men, he must have had extrasensory perception into the 20th century and focused in on Ravitch/Lauder/Cohen *et al.*

The tender concern that the Supreme Court evinced in applying the First Amendment to the rights of pornographers to pollute the minds of the current and future generations, also caused some anxiety to Lauder, Cohen and partners, and to Ravitch as well. The porno shops, massage parlors and allied trades had taken an even greater hold on the surrounding area. The question of who would pay $100 per room per month in that run-down and dangerous area became exacerbated by these new developments.

How Mitchell-Lama is financed

The $90 million that the city had undertaken to give to Ravitch as a mortgage on Manhattan Plaza was not to come out of the city's treasury. Rather, the city went to the banks to borrow the money at the then-going rates of interest that the city then re-lends to the developer. Since the income-tax laws make interest earned on state and municipal obligations nontaxable, the city in this case can borrow at a cheaper rate than could a private mortgagor. The theory is that this device should hold down rents.

In 1967, when Ravitch got his okay from the city, interest rates on city bonds were less than 4% and had been even lower in previous years. The city officials and their hired and well-paid financial advisers decided that this rate of interest was not only too high, but was also temporary and would fall to lower levels in the near future.

Acting on this clairvoyant insight, they borrowed the $90 millions on short-term notes (one or two years). They would, when interest rates fell again, pick up these short-term notes and reissue in their place long-term 40-year bonds at lower interest rates.

But that did not happen. Instead, interest rates continued upward. The city (in 1976-77) was paying an average of 7.66% on short-term notes and 8%, at least, on long-term bonds. It is calculated that a 1% jump in interest rates adds $13 per room to the monthly rent in Manhattan Plaza.

On this basis, the stated debt service (principal and interest) would take, as its part of the rent, $110 to $115 per room per month. With other costs, which also had risen, the new rent requirements were $150 to $160 per month per room. Therefore, rents would have to range from a low of $375 per month for an efficiency unit to $750 for the two-bedroom with balcony apartment.

A big bust in the making

No one close to the project could argue that such rentals were obtainable. And a huge bust was in prospect.

Ravitch, who had made a sizable profit, had nothing to lose. In fact, while all this was going on, he continued his constuction skyward and was raking in his overhead and profit and whatever else was possible. Lauder *et al.*, on the other hand, had a stake of $12 million, which, if they lost all, would end up as a $9 million loss after tax write-offs. But the City of New York was in, at the time, for $65 million, and the full $90 million when the building was completed.

Section 8 to the rescue

Of all the options open to it (and they were numerous), each of which would entail losses to all but Ravitch, the city decided to opt for Section 8 to salvage this mess. Section 8 of the Housing and Community Development Act of 1974 is the federal program which subsidizes all rents over 25% of income (in some cases, over 15% of income) for eligible tenants. Schur calls this the ". . . most costly and expensive housing subsidy program yet invented by the fertile brains of the housing industry and the United States Congress."

Under Section 8, the apartments would be rented out at $150-$160 per room. The tenants would pay 25% of income (or 15%), and the balance of the rent would be paid out of federal subsidy money. This would cost $11½ million to $12 million per year—or 16% of the $75 million of Section 8 money allocated to the entire City of New York—for this one project alone! The federal law continues this subsidy for 40 years, which in this case coincides with the entire period of the Mitchall-Lama mortgage.

Now, let us see just what this option really means.

• This subsidy, over the 40-year lifetime, multiplied by 1,698 apartments, would cost at least $460 million to the U.S. taxpayer.

• To this $460 million must be added another approximately $25 million lost in taxes through the Lauder *et al.* tax shelters, so that the total taxpayer cost is $485 million, almost one-half a billion dollars over the 40-year period.

• Divide this by 1,698 apartments and by 40 years, and the cost of Section 8 subsidy becomes $7,300 per year, or $608 per month per apartment, which, it is estimated, is about 4 times the rental of the average New York household.

• If the building were to be rented to average people at $47 per room (the cost of running the building without debt service charges), taking the loss of $90 million, this would be only one-fifth the total cost to the taxpayers of the Section 8 cost of $460 million.

• If the building were allowed to stay uncompleted and empty, it would cost the city "only" $90 million.

It is clear that from the point of view of the taxpayer or just plain sensible economics, it is the worst option possible!

The cover-up
But from the point of view of covering up the city's mess,

making good to the Ravitch/Lauder/real estate buddies, who, after all make the contributions that in turn make election victories possible, and also from the point of view of not having to take a loss that year and thus face public wrath and acrimony, it was deemed better to let the next generation pay five times as much as any sensible solution would cost.

From here on out, the story has elements of drama, ingenuity, some comedy—but the economics by now are complete.

Ravitch and Durst had a falling out on what Section 8 people would do to Durst's hopes of upgrading his surrounding properties. So a scheme was concocted to make Manhattan Plaza a project for the glamorous theatrical trades. This was done and the neighborhood saved from "those people"—the poor—who thoughtlessly and selfishly drive down real estate values.

One postscript and our story is done. The City of New York hovers close to the edge of bankruptcy. The question "why?" can be answered by knowing that many, if not most, of the city's decisions and budget allocations are made on the moral level of those outlined in this Manhattan Plaza saga.

The bankers' role

The very moral bankers, who had themselves disposed of most of their New York City bond and note holdings to an unwary public, are pushing the city precariously closer to the precipice. They have refused to refinance the maturing short-term notes that the city so blithely issued, and have imposed a banker dictatorship, called the Municipal Assistance Corporation, over the city's financial and budgetary affairs. As the notes come due the city must scramble for funds to meet them or go over the edge to bankruptcy.

With the same deference to their real estate/banking masters, the city fathers devised a scheme to meet this emergency. They are selling their Mitchell-Lama mortgages to private industry at the bargain rates of 35 cents to 40 cents on the dollar. This gives the city quick cash; temporarily staves off bankruptcy; gives real estate/banking a big bargain; puts the Mitchell-Lama tenants in even greater jeopardy than before, and turns over to the next generation the reaping of the currently generated whirlwind.

Note on Manhattan Plaza: While the city has made no announcement regarding the sale of the Manhattan Plaza mortgage (probably because the project is as yet unfinished and only partly rented as this is written in June 1977), it is probable that at the most propitious time it will do so. To all the other losses (meaning burden to the taxpayers) should be added the following: If the $90 million mortgage is sold for 35 cents on the dollar, the loss to the city will be $58,500,000. If it is sold at 40 cents on the dollar, the loss will be $54 million.

The why of shoddy construction

Mitchell-Lama projects are almost invariably shoddy in construction. Almost every one of them have structural or construction defects or equipment faults. For example:

• At Gouverneur Gardens, complete plumbing systems had to be replaced in two of the buildings. Windows do not work and terraces are sagging dangerously.

• At Esplanade Gardens, the bulkhead at the garage fell into the Harlem River. The repair costs were $500,000.

Governor Carey appointed a task force to inquire into Mitchell-Lama defects and irregularities. Met Council's Mitchell-Lama Committee appeared before this task force on February 25th, 1977.

Here are some of the "irregularities" in her complex of buildings that were reported by Franklin Plaza Board Member, Natalie Williams.

	Cost of repairs
Water seepage through brick work into apartments	$ 30,000
Falling bricks from sides of building	21,000
Salt water from East River entering heating system due to improperly cradled steam pipes under Second Avenue, and laid in the marsh instead, cost of tube replacement, welding and cradling	50,000
Additional cost of damaged heating equipment	50,000

Fuel oil wasted in order to heat cold water entering system through above cracks	$300,000
Using odd lot tiles, which no can longer be bought, to replace those worn out	per year 25,000
Faulty incinerator chambers (re-building costs)	3,400
Extra heavy lobby doors, which are difficult to open, replacements	26,000
Defective entrance canopies	7,000
No drainage system in basement for floods, etc.	100,000
Parking lots, walk ways, and side walks are caving in	500,000
Total cost: above items	$1,112,400

These items are indicative, not complete.

This list can be expanded to include almost every Mitchell-Lama project—and to include the most serious of needs, ranging from leaking roofs to defective elevators, to heating systems that break down, to inadequate insulation, to poorly hung doors and windows, and so on into infinity.

Why, by this time, is not hard to answer. Mitchell-Lama is called housing—but it is really a giant pork-barrel for all connected with it except the tenants.

As can be seen from the foregoing, especially the Manhattan Plaza analysis, the reason for investing in real estate is to make a quick buck, faster than elsewhere. In less than four years, Lauder/Cohen had returned to them all their investment. The next four, five, or six years are all profit and tax shelter. At about this time, they will sell to another tax-shelter seeker, and reap a capital gain, taxable at half the rate of ordinary income.

This is the full and entire meaning of housing—Manhattan Plaza type housing, that is—to the investors. It does not matter to them if the tenants are miserable from lack of services or even if the building collapses in a heap. They've had theirs and now they are out of it.

And the builder has essentially the same attitude, with minor variations on the theme. He can substitute whitewash for plaster, put more sand than cement in the mix, get the cheapest elevators, cut corners on labor and save millions for himself. The owners won't be the owners for long, so they don't care. Of course, there are plans and specifications—but who looks at them? The architects must do as they are told, or risk no more work. The inspectors, as the newspapers tell us, are paid off to look the other way. And the city, who is in it from the beginning, does not prosecute.

The results are as described—indescribable!

Federal pre-emption

It has been demonstrated in the many facts, statistics and analyses that have preceded, that real estate/banking is neither poverty-stricken nor in the remotest danger of becoming so in the foreseeable future. Quite the contrary. Despite its being "shackled" with rent controls or rent stabilization in parts of New York State or with the various forms of controls that exist in some other areas of the country, real estate/banking is making quite fabulous (not too strong a word) profits.

Yet it remains discontent. It ceaselessly fights to eliminate controls; and when it cannot do so completely, it tries to diminsh them. Where it can, it does it legislatively. Where it cannot, it does so administratively. through some of its many servants, who assume a neutral guise but perform well for their masters. The Metropolitan Council on Housing has a file called "Where They Come From —Where They Go." A few examples of those who are involved with housing administration are enlightening.

> Paul Belica, former Executive Director of the New York State Housing Finance Agency since 1963, has joined the investment banking firm of Smith Barney, Harris Upham & Co.

> *(New York Times,* March 2, 1977)

Albert Walsh, former Administrator of New York City's Housing and Development Administration, resigned to become President of the National Realty Committee, a nationwide lobbying organization of property owners and real estate investor.

(SoHo Weekly, April 17, 1975)

[His salary is reputed to be $75,000 per year.]

Charles Urstadt, the author of the New York State law that removes from the City of New York its right to enact laws that may correct inequities or even gross injustices against tenants, was New York State Commissioner of Housing and Community Renewal until he resigned in April of 1973. He formerly was with Alcoa Corporation as attorney in charge of real estate, and attempted to evict the tenant leaders of Lincoln Towers, who had recently organized.

(Daily World, April 11, 1973)

After resigning, the *Real Estate Weekly* reported that he [Urstadt] had purchased a major interest in Douglas L. Elliman & Co., a large New York City real estate concern.

(New York Times, April 6, 1973)

Since the machinery at all levels of government is real estate/banking oriented, the real estate industry is able to operate on many governmental fronts. When it finds resistance at the local level temporarily too strong to overcome, it moves to the state level, where tenant pressure is more difficult to apply. When it finds the state government unable or unwilling to fulfill all its demands, it moves on to the ultimate and remotest power, the federal government.

One of Nelson Rockefeller's last gestures of good will to his fellow landlords, before retiring as Governor of the State of New York, was to sire the Vacancy Decontrol Law. As its name implies, when a rent-controlled or rent-stabilized apartment became vacant, all controls ceased and the landlord was free to demand any rents he saw fit to ask.

In the three-year period before the present minimal curb was attached to vacancy decontrol, rents in vacated apartments rose by 100%, 200%, 300% and, in some rare cases, even more. The outrage was such that Rockefeller's successor, Governor Malcolm Wilson, was compelled to demand that the legislature re-enact some form of control, lest the ensuing scandal force him from office. There resulted a weak hodge-podge called the Emergency Tenant Protection Act.

Such an experience makes it clear that landlords cannot totally rely on even their well-disposed state officials.

In relentless pursuit of its unfettered goal, real estate/banking moved on to Washington, D.C., and its friends at the Department of Housing and Urban Development (HUD). At this level, any outrage is safer. The overwhelming majority of the nation is not rent-controlled. The majority does not even live as tenants in multifamily buildings. The Secretary of HUD does not have to be elected. So, here is their woman, Secretary Carla Hills, a Ford appointee.

On February 26, 1975, there was published in the *Federal Register*, regulation #403. This regulation empowers HUD to pre-empt the authority of any local or state agency or existing local legislation, in buildings that either have mortgages insured by the federal government or are subsidized by it, in situations where HUD deems its subsidies or mortgage insurance or interests to be in jeopardy.

In such cases HUD pre-empts and supersedes all existing state and local regulations, laws, limitations or controls.

There are certain formalistic "due process" procedures that are required, but in reality they are quite meaningless.

The landlord is required to file with the appropriate local agency an application for what he deems to be the amount of "hardship" increase that is needed to meet the expense requirements of his building.

The local agency has just 30 days in which to respond favorably to that application. If it does not, the landlord files with HUD a form—which is a self-serving, unaudited statement of his "economic jeopardy."

HUD thereupon is empowered to grant an increase—*in any amount*—based on the difference between the landlords' expenses and the rent roll.

It should be noted at the outset that the constitutionally required due process is apparently reserved only for the landlord and the local agency. There is no due process for the tenant. He or she is not notified that an application is being filed, not even if the consequences of the approval of such an application may result in economic disaster. The tenant is not given given the due process of a response to what may be either untruths or distortions of fact or the absence of certain facts in the landlord's application.

A "due process" gesture is made to the local regulatory agency that is about to be superseded. They have all of 30 days to grant the landlord's demand—an impossibly short period of time. Should the facts furnished prove inadequate or contradictory, there is hardly time for a letter and a response to it. There is no time for a hearing or an independent investigation as to the veracity of the statements contained in the application. Certainly the tenants at the local level could hardly begin to organize their reply, let alone analyze the landlord's allegations and prepare a response to them.

It is obviously an empty bow in the direction of the constitution; a statement of "we know it is there, but will nevertheless do what we would have done if it were not there." It underscores the deeply ingrained landlord/banking prejudice that motivates these agencies at every turn of events.

But away from constitutional "guarantees." Let us get to the substance of this pre-emption. Let us deal with its economics.

In the previous section we have analyzed what we have termed a classic subsidized housing example. The details may—indeed will—vary from project to project, but the essence will remain invariable and constant. What are the important invariables?

Two of them are interest rates and mortgage-principal re-payments. In our Manhattan Plaza example we saw that debt service cost $113* per month per room while all other costs came to $47 per month per room—for a total cost of $160 per month per room. That is to say, debt service cost 70.6% and all other costs constituted 29.4% of the rent dollar.

Is it not clear from this one fact that if HUD were looking for a way to prevent default or deficit operations by a landlord, it would seek to control or restructure the 70.6% area of cost? This is where the real money goes. Why not try to find a way to contain it?

---

*The approximate average of the $110 to $115 debt-service cost.

That it makes no such attempt, even an empty gesture in this direction, is to underscore what all the facts and logic of this document scream out at us: that real estate/banking *and the government*, as its dependable ally, *use* housing, build and operate it, in order to maximize profits and not to shelter human beings.

It will be seen in a later section of this book that interest rates are extortionate and usurious. Interest rates can be, should be, and indeed have been one-third or less than present rates. And that happened so recently in our history that it is not possible that our HUD administrators could have either forgotten it or buried it so deeply in their bureaucratic files that they cannot research it. It happened only 40 years ago.

As to the other aspect of debt service, the amortization of the mortgage principal: Again referring to our Manhattan Plaza example, we saw there how a mortgage is ballooned up to an unstable, financially impossible but highly profitable monstrosity. It started with a $7 million overnight profit by Ravitch. This became part of the mortgage. It then went on through the listing of all the large and sundry allowable "costs" that also became part of the mortgage.

Let us do some arithmetic. The total cost of Manhattan Plaza is $102 million. Ravitch's HRH Construction Company got $60 million for construction in costs, profit and overhead. That left $42 million in all sorts of costs, both real and imagined. Let us here be arbitrary but not too unrealistic. If we presume that $20 million of this $42 million was waste, graft, unseen and totally unnecessary profit, then the mortgage would have been only $82 million. If again we deduct Ravitch's $7 million overnight bonanza, the mortgage would be only $75 million, a mortgage reduction of $27 million or 26.5%.

If we apply this 26.5% to the $113 per room per month of debt-service cost—because indeed the mortgage should have been that much less—we find that the debt service cost per room per month is reduced by $29.95 per room per month and thus becomes $83.05. The rental of $160 per room per month suddenly falls to $130.05.

While this is not our idea of the ideal rental rate per room, it is nevertheless a far cry from $160, and it is caused by the application of an adjustment to only one item, that is, mortgage principal.

As to interest, it is obvious what that would do. A 1% drop in interest rates equals $13 per room per month. In 1976-77 the New York City average interest rate on its tax-exempt bonds was 7.66%. If this were reduced to a completely viable 3%, the savings would be 4.66% or $60.58 per room per month.

Deducting from our $130.05 rate per room per month, obtained by the correction of mortgage principal, the savings of $60.58 by a proper interest rate, we suddenly find ourselves with a room rate rental of $69.47. This begins to put it in the area of middle income affordability, although it is by no means at the limits of where no more corrupt dollars can be squeezed from it.

But there is no need to go further. Our point is that if HUD is motivated to act to protect its investments in subsidies or in insurance or the general interests of the federal government, as it says it is, they need not look further afield. It is all here, more than enough to remove any "hardship" claim from any landlord's application. On the contrary, not only can rents be reduced, but the government's subsidies can be removed or at least substantially lessened.

We have seen in previous sections the relationship between capital gains and rents. As need hardly be stated, the federal government does not prohibit a landlord from selling government-insured or subsidized buildings to another landlord. It certainly does not prevent him from selling at a profit—even a huge one.

By this process the new landlord, having a larger investment and a bigger mortgage, needs more rent to pay for the return on his investment and the interest and principal of his larger mortgage.

If the existing cash-flow puts the new owner in "jeopardy," HUD will then permit whatever increase is necessary to save the federal government from the necessity of taking over the "jeopardized" building in foreclosure.

So here we have every encouragement to a speed-up of the profit-from-operations to the capital-gains cycle engendered by the ever higher rents at each turn of the cycle, each new resale of the building. Thus the more the capital gains profit, the more the profit from operations and of course the more the rent paid by the tenant.

It is clear that HUD has decided that either the tenant has limitless capacity to pay ever higher rents or, alternatively, that HUD is embarked on the conscious and deliberate policy of bankrupting and utterly impoverishing the tenants of the United States. There is no third alternative. No other interpretation is possible.

We have also seen in previous sections that landlords milk buildings dry and, having thus made their superprofits, abandon them and the tenants along with the buildings. This process is not one to inspire confidence in the integrity of landlords. We have then seen how some of them, driven by the additional profits to be obtained, torch or have others torch for them, the abandoned building for the insurance. Not even the various Real Estate Boards can publicly condone this process as ethical.

Yet HUD accepts without question, and without the tenants' ability to reply or rebut the unsworn, unaudited statement by landlords, even of the two types described above, that they need rent increases and are in "jeopardy." It cannot be naiveté. It therefore must be deliberate, conscious and, one may even say, with malice aforethought.

In summary:

1) Landlords will not build new low- and middle-income housing and thereby have created a shortage.
2) The shortage forces rents to a higher level.
3) The sale and resale of neglected buildings at higher prices is made possible because:
    a) The tenants have nowhere to go.
    b) Each resale again brings with it higher rents.
4) When this process begins to reach the point of no return, that is, when tenants have no more money to pay for rent,
5) Landlords, Real Estate Boards and the media spokesmen, with the great ardor of public do-gooders, demand:
    a) Government subsidies of private housing, because people cannot pay the "economic" rent, and

    b) Government insurance for housing grown too fiscally unstable, with the constant boosting of the costs or resale values, for banks to risk their own money for mortgages. (The interest rates remain undiminished even though the mortgages now are without one cent of risk.)

6) When this process is in motion and is ingrained as public policy with no mass organized or articulate opposition, they then take the next step:

7) The very reason for the institution of government subsidy to privately owned housing and government insurance of privately owned housing is now twisted by 180 degrees and becomes the new reason for additional rent increases and the removal of all local controls, lest the government be forced to foreclose on the properties it subsidized or insured!

Perhaps this section should close on the vibrant, ringing, patriotic and fervent note of the editorial in the *Real Estate Weekly* of April 10, 1975. It is quoted in full. The emphasis is ours.

"Washington to the Rescue?

The federal government has finally given some recognition to the economic disaster of rent control by disclosing that it will try to override local controls if they're jeopardizing the operation of apartment houses with federally-insured mortgages.

Although this program will affect only a small number of buildings in New York, it might finally pave the way for long-overdue federal intervention into the whole rent control mess.

Billions of dollars and millions of lives have been spent defending freedom around the world—and they most assuredly were not spent to perpetuate a system of property confiscation. If Washington would recognize rent control for what it is, maybe the nightmare would finally end."

Why don't more people go into real estate?

Having described in so much detail the almost unbelievable profits that landlords make (mostly unknown to the public), one is inclined to ask why don't more people go into it?

For one thing, most people—and all decent people—don't have the stomach for it.

Here is a quotation from *The Handbook of Real Estate Investment* by Don. G. Campbell. The author is explaining who should and who should not take the plunge into real estate.

> "The sight is enough to tear the heart right out of the stoniest breast: our hero's small son—a normally bonny child—bursts into the house awash with tears of humiliation. 'Daddy! Daddy!' he sobs pitifully. 'Some kids down at school say that you're a . . . a . . .' He gropes painfully for the word. 'They say you're a . . . a speculator!' If this is the sort of thing that grabs you and throws you into a deep funk perhaps you'll be happier in the wholesale poultry business."

Here we have it straight from a real estate spokesman. But that is not really all. A worthy landlord can either handle or ignore his delicate child.

The fact is that not everyone can win. Not in a horse race, a lottery, in the grocery business nor in real estate. There is this thing known as competition. There is also this thing known as the drive for limitless accumulation. Do Rockefeller, Ford, Getty or Hughes have enough? In business there is no such thing as enough. For if you don't get—and stay—stronger than your competitor, he'll take it away from you, whereas if you keep on top you can take it away from him.

It follows therefore that someones has to lose, someone has to be lowest on the totem pole. It may be because he is not smart enough. It may also be that he is not ruthless enough.

Take, for example, the late William Zeckendorf, Sr., whose vast real estate empire collapsed a few years ago. It could not be said of him that he was neither smart nor ruthless. He had enough of both of these qualities. But luck ran out; he spread himself too thin; too much leveraging; too many properties. The cash flow income hesitated a bit too long. The banks and other creditors demanded theirs. He could not raise enough money quickly enough to hold them off. The other wolves rushed in to foreclose on his properties or to make him sell at bargain rates in order to gain enough cash to hold off the other creditors. The vast upside-down pyramid began to topple. And William Zeckendorf went to the lower reaches of the totem pole.

So landlords, too, must know their way around this very sharp and competitive industry. They have to be able to fend off this creditor and that banker for such a period of time—precisely because the landlords have *leverage*. Leverage translated into plain business English means too little capital is invested and the landlord is spread too thin.

So the meeker, the less sharp, the unluckier, but especially the smaller ones, go down the drain. Sorry! Real estate is not for the average person.

Real estate cannot and will not build for low- and middle-income people

The current housing shortage—How and why

World War II was a golden opportunity for landlords. With the decision to shift all production to war requirements, virtually no housing was built from 1942 to 1945. To aggravate this condition, the influx of large numbers of people came to the bigger cities to work in the vastly expanded war industries. The result was no vacancies (previously landlords figured on a 10% or 20% vacancy rate). But rents were held in place, as were the prices of all goods and services, by wartime price controls. When the war was over, landlords were besieged with requests for nonavailable apartments. This was a delightful position to be in except for the damnable rent-control laws.

Quick to recognize a good thing when they saw it, landlords "decided" to keep new construction well behind demand and to use the power of the shortage to gain profits as well as to exert pressure for governmental relief from rent controls. And relief they did get, in the form of across-the-board increases, increases for new tenants as well as administrative relaxation of the laws, diminution of services and many more landlord advantages.

The campaign to abolish rent controls took on new power with each passing year. Meanwhile, with rents going up, the capital value of real estate increased; large and quick profits could be made in buying and selling. In fact, more money could be made that way than by constructing new housing, and with much less investment and fewer headaches.

In this atmosphere of shortage and with large under-the-table payments for apartments made vacant by moves to the suburbs or by death, all real estate was booming—Park Avenue and the ghetto as well. So why build? Trade instead. Keep the shortage, reduce the services and up the rents and profits!

Increase in "Capital Value" and effect on new construction

We have seen from our discussion "Effects of Capital Gains on the Tenant" (page 9) that the purchase of a building by a new landlord at a higher price resulted in higher rents.

It is now over 30 years since the end of World War II and there have been many real estate booms. Translated into the simple terms of its effect on the population, boom means: capital gains profit for the landlord, higher rents for the tenant, multiplying this process 10 or 20 times over, thereby pushing the market in rentals to qualitatively new, higher and more disastrous levels. A case in point: A reasonably new and well-cared-for apartment that rented in 1945 for $80 a month is now marketed for $200 to $300 per month or more.

If the rental is at this rate, then it follows that the capital value has increased proportionately. Let us say the rental above has increased 300%. Applying this to the $1 million building in our previous examples, the capital value is now $3 million.

If interest rates remained the same, and they decidedly did not (more about this later), then the cost of constructing the $80-per-month apartment, which might have been $15,000 in 1945, suddenly becomes $45,000.

We have read many times in the press about what has happened to the new construction market. We have heard about labor costs and brick and mortar costs. While it is true that the costs of labor and materials have risen in this period, these are not, by a long shot, the main or determining factors in construction costs. Not even the rise in real estate taxes is basically important.

Going back to the MBR formula (page 14), the major factor is "Return on Capital Value," which takes 42.4% of the rent dollar. This critically affects the rising cash capital now required to be invested and the rising amount of money to be borrowed on mortgages.

If the interest rate remained the same (which it does not), than the amount of interest paid increased by 300%. If the amortization period is the same (and this is probably so), then the amount of principal payment has risen by 300%. If the *rate* of profit that the landlord is content with remains the same, then the *amount* of profit has increased by 300%.

Interest rates

However, the *interest rates decidedly did not remain the same.* In the 1945 period, a mortgage rate of 5% (or less) was the going rate. It has now almost doubled. That would make the interest factor increase from 300% to 600%.

Prior to World War II, when the income taxes levied on low- and middle-income people were very low or nonexistent, rent was supposed to consume considerably less than 25% of income. With the huge rent increases that have taken place in recent years, rents have gone up to 35%, 40% and even 50% of wages. Old people on social security have been known to pay 60% of their income for rent while forced to eat dog food.

If housing has priced itself out of the market, then the reasons for it are not labor or materials but profit—all three kinds, capital, operating and interest.

While interest charges are one item of a dozen or so in the list of housing costs, it is not generally known that interest is the *main* item of cost. In 1971 it was determined that about 50 cents of every rent dollar went to the payment of charges that were mainly interest, technically called debt service. (*New York Times,* July 25, 1971.) Since it is now five years later, and interest rates have risen, debt service has undoubtedly risen even further. So, here we have the main culprit. *If debt service were eliminated, our rents could be cut in half.* Likewise, the cost of constructing a new building would be cut in half.

Landlords have priced themselves out of the low- and middle-income markets

Big landlords and government-housing spokesmen have stated openly and with increasing frequency that they cannot build housing for low- and middle-income people. As the then Administrator of the New York City Housing and Development Administration, Roger Starr predicted,

> "Traditional apartments are not going to be built without federal subsidies."
>
> (*New York Post,* September 8, 1976)

The economic reasons for this have previously been outlined. The key word in the quoted statement is "subsidies," while "traditional" is the code word for low and middle income.

Thus it becomes the problem for landlords and their theoreticians to devise a program that will, as long as the house of cards stands up, keep a roof over the heads of the low- and middle-income people who have exhausted their last resource and at the same time accelerate the upward flow of profit and rising rents. What else but to dip into that bottomless pit, the U.S. Treasury?

Rent Supplements

Landlords argue with their own supreme logic that if poor and middle-income tenants cannot pay more, landlords cannot build more. Since people have to live somewhere, the government should supplement the rents of these tenants by paying to the landlord the difference between what the tenant can afford and the "economic" rents which the landlords require.

(As used by real estate/banking, the word "economic" means "take us out of the mess we have created.")

That the landlords have initially succeeded in this line is attested to by the passage and implementation of Section 8. (See page 37.) Undoubtedly they will receive more subsidies and handouts—the application of Section 8 has only just begun.

It is an ingenious process and not a little ironic that poor tenants have to pay more in income and other taxes so that the government can hand this over to the landlords to help pay the rents that tenants cannot afford to pay!

The main result of these manipulations by real estate/banking is the general and continued impoverishment of ever growing segments of the U.S. population.

While rent and other prices go steadily upward at a fast pace (at least 6% per year—and as high as 12% some years), wages rise at a much slower pace. The gap between prices and wages constitutes the degree of people's impoverishment.

The additional amounts paid in rent force a reduced living standard—less and cheaper food, less and poorer clothing, or skimping on medical and dental care (or doing without), reduced higher or even intermediate education for the children, and less or no cultural or entertainment spending, as well as the reduction or elimination of all amenities.

Also we find an increasing incidence of doubled-up families, and of grown or married children continuing to live with their parents because they are priced out of their own homes.

Role of the banks

Domination of the economy

The banks (and insurance companies) own the vast majority of American wealth. What they do not literally own, they control through mortgages, loans, managing pension-fund portfolios, and the portfolios of wealthy private investors and trusts. In addition, they float and manage bond issues and lend money to city, county and state as well as to the federal government.

The money which the banks lend is, of course, not their own, except that portion which they have managed to siphon off to themselves over the years. The money is, in large measure, the life savings of each us, multiplied by 215 million people, With no consultation, the bankers decide who shall receive loans, who shall not; what industries are to be protected, which rejected; who shall be provided favored treatment, who shall go bankrupt.

Who are these people? Are they known to us? Do we elect them? Can we remove them? How did they get there?

They are a handful of members of the boards of directors of the banks.

It is common knowledge that a numerically small group of very wealthy stockholders controls and dominates a public company's affairs by owning 3% to 5% of the outstanding shares of that corporation (or voting the proxies of others). They can and do elect the board of directors and decide its policies.

Even the above "democratic" procedures do not apply to the so-called mutual savings banks and insurance companies. They were originally chartered to a handful of organizers, the boards of directors. From then on the boards of directors are self-perpetuating. One board member dies or retires and the remainder elect a substitute. They are responsible to no one but themselves.

The banks, through their power of life and death over the corporations, to whom they lend endless millions or billions of dollars, are thus able to designate one or more members of the boards of directors of these corporations. The bank-designated members are the key members, the "powerhouses." Their influence or decisions count, or else loans are called or not renewed.

When the City of New York has to finance or refinance a loan, a combination of banks, or syndicate, makes a bid as to the interest to be charged. In recent years, only one bid has been submitted. Take it or leave it! So the City pays whatever the bankers say—and it becomes a de facto part of our taxes.

This was the invisible power behind our governments (city, state, federal) until recently. When the combination of legal banking usury and other corruptions brought our city to the edge of disaster, the banks decided that the elected officials should be superseded by a set of the banks' designees, who, they said, were more efficient and better managers. So now the visible government is the Municipal Assistance Corporation (MAC) and the Emergency Financial Control Board (EFCB) on the state level.

The results of this changing of the guard over our fiscal problems can be judged by a few facts:

• The first MAC bond issues, at the banks' insistence, sold at an interest rate of 11% instead of 7%, 8% or 9% (tax-exempt, of course). This means that in about nine years we will have paid in interest the total amount of the bond issue while still continuing to owe the full amount! This is our legacy to the next generation.

• Many thousands of teachers, firemen, police, sanitation workers, day-care teachers, social service workers, and other categories of needed city workers, were fired, but *the interest rates paid to the banks went even higher.*

The sword of Damocles that the banks hang over the head of New York City is likewise suspended over all cities, all counties, all states and, indeed, the United States government. The interest rates that are paid on U.S. Treasury bills, notes and bonds are determined by the banks, who make the market.

Even the national financial policies are determined, officially, by the banks. They are the decisive force, and they designate the most powerful officials of the Federal Reserve System. Once appointed, the chairmen of the Federal Reserve Banks and their boards are independent of both Congress and the President of the United States in their financial and fiscal decision-making.

The banks and real estate

The banks are the decisive force behind real estate. As we have previously seen, loans by the banks constitute 90% or so of real estate costs.

This is not a social service that they perform for the good of the country. It is for profit.

And profit has many faces. There is the legitimate face, such as interest on the mortgage; the semi-legitimate face, such as demanding a seat on the board of directors; and the illegitimate ones that abound in such numbers they are impossible to record.

Some examples: "Jones, Jones, Jones and Smith are excellent lawyers and have done their clients much good"; "did you ever think of using the ABC Construction Company to erect your building?"; "buy your steel, plumbing, etc. from so-and-so"; "there is a good friend who can be very useful to you—he really should be your partner (general manager, etc.)." Of course, we state it crudely. Bankers are never crude. They almost never say anything that, quoted or even tape-recorded, is incriminating. But they do make their point and their gentlest suggestions are either accepted or somehow the loan is slow to come; or there are many problems that crop up; or the ratio of current assets to current liabilities is less than fully desirable, etc., etc.

The man who wants the loan or mortgage gets the point and, unless he knows someone who will make a deal for less, he goes along or goes under.

Leonard Downie, Jr., in his book, *Mortgage on America*, has documented some of the vast corruption that exists in land speculation, financing and government giveaways. He speaks, for example, of two presidents of savings and loan associations in the same city, who, prohibited by law from approving loans for themselves or their companies, simply arranged to make loans to each other's companies.

Interest rates and their justification

Interest rates were intended to serve certain banking needs. The most obvious are:

- cost of running the bank (payroll, operations, etc.),
- building a reserve account to make up for some inevitable losses,
- providing a profit for the stockholders.

Without dwelling on the first and last reasons, let us examine the role of the second one.

Judgments being what they are, some mistakes are bound to happen, and unless the interest charged on loans and mortgages is high enough to provide a sufficiently large reserve, bankruptcy will inevitably result. Given the framework of the banking system, who can quarrel with that concept?

Federal Guaranteed Mortgages

More and more since World War II, the government (mainly federal, but state and city as well) has stepped in with our tax money and has responded to the landlords' cries of "We can't make it," and "We need help or we can't build."

The responses have been endless. We have dealt with a few of them earlier. One type in particular—guaranteed mortgages—deserves our attention. These guaranteed mortgages are issued by the Federal Housing Administration and the Veterans Administration.

A guaranteed mortgage means, in effect, that if the landlord fails to pay, the government will—not only the principal of the mortgage but the accumulated interest as well.

Thus, the bank has *no risks*. It need not keep part of the interest charges as a reserve against losses. It needs only ½% or so for administrative expense, and whatever, for profit.

But the bank nevertheless charges all the market will bear. It charges the full 9% or 9½%, plus all the extra points, plus sundry under-the-table devices, plus requiring the maintenance of a certain high unused bank balance or non interest-bearing certificates of deposit.

There is no conceivable justification for the current interest rates on guaranteed mortgages, unless limitless profit is a justification in itself.

The reverse side of this coin is equally negative. To the extent that there is no risk involved, the bank does not really care if the building under mortgage is managed well or poorly, well-built or shoddy, useful or useless. The bank will get its money from the U.S. Treasury in any case.

This means that the builder may submit a budget of one million dollars and get a loan based on that amount, but by substituting poorer materials and, by cutting quality (using one coat of paint instead of two, for example), he may spend $800,000 and pocket the difference or perhaps share it with the bank's representative or with bribed inspectors.

There is no fantasy nor a theoretical situation. One case in point: In a Mitchell-Lama development, Lindsay Park, in Brooklyn, where 3,000 ceilings have fallen, no one is to blame—not the builder, the architect, the sponsor, the subcontractors—no one. No one has been jailed, no one fined. But the tenant cooperators, who were sold this planned lemon, have to live in this mess or find money to rebuild it.

There are few government giveaways that go directly to the recipient. The banks always interpose themselves. Everything must go through them so they can get their cut.

For example, on the theory that rents could be held down, Sections 236 and 221 (d) (3) of the Federal Housing Law reduce interest rates to 1% and 3%, respectively. But did the government advance the money to the builder and charge him these rates? No. Instead, the builder arranged for the guaranteed loans from a bank at the market interest rates, and the government picked up the difference between market rates and the 1% or 3% burden that we the taxpayers must bear.

Red-lining, block-busting, and ghettoizing

These practices of red-lining, block-busting and ghettoizing are, in essence, decisions on the part of the banks not to lend money for mortgages in areas which they decide are to be allowed to decay; no new construction, no rehabilitation, and no home-improvement loans for the private homes in these areas. Areas like this exist in the South Bronx, in the Brownsville section of Brooklyn, the Lower East Side and Harlem in Manhattan, and throughout the city and country. These practices go hand-in-hand with the movement of Black people and other minorities out of their narrowly confined, dilapidated, high-rent areas to slightly better ones.

This process, too, is a way of making money. It raises the rents because new housing is not constructed. It causes decay and abandonment, out of which many real estate fortunes have been built.

When an area is so decimated after a few years that it resembles a wartime bombed-out city, and after the profit-making abandonment process is relatively completed, as in the South Bronx, along comes a real estate spokesman, whether or not disguised as a city official (such as the former HDA Administrator Roger Starr) and proposes that all city services, including police, fire, sanitation, etc. be withdrawn (perhaps the residents will melt away). He calls it "planned shrinkage." *(Real Estate Weekly,* February 9, 1976.)

Felix Rohatyn of the Municipal Assistance Corporation "believes some tracts of ravaged residential property around the city could be cleared for industrial development." *(New York Post,* March 17, 1976.)

After a while, real estate prices are depressed, at which point a syndicate of speculators buys up the land cheaply, has the area re-zoned for high-price residential or commercial or manufacturing use, and begins a new cycle of making profits from that area.

That the banks are the principal perpetrators has been demonstrated time and again. They indeed are the *main malefactors*, the main despoilers of the lives of the common man and woman in this country.

What should interest rates be?

We have seen that interest rates (debt service) consume 50% to 60% of the rent dollar. At 9% to 9½% (second mortgages—15% to 20%), the effect is not only calamitous, but it is economically impossible to adapt it to the budgets of the low- and middle-income earners that make up some 90% of our population. It seriously affects our health and life, violently deforming the economy and social structure of our country.

In the period 1955 to 1960, as a case in point, mortgages could be had for about 5%. Why did they double? Is there a subtle, invisible but irresistible, economic cause for this rise? None! There are only the bankers' decisions and the profit pressures.

In the depression years of 1929 and the subsequent 1930's, President Roosevelt reduced mortgage interest to 3% and less. Not only did the banks not fail, but those that wobbled were stabilized. That is to say, they made a profit, they continued to function.

As reported in the *New York Times*, May 19, 1976, "Interest rates were as low as 2 percent to 3 percent prior to World War II. They generally averaged 4% to 7% during the middle-income housing boom following the war and climbed to as high as 9% during the credit squeeze in 1974."

There is no more reason to pay more than 3% today than there was in the 1930's. The economy, industry, housing and the people would all be the healthier for a 3% interest rate.

As we have previously stated, an interest rate of ½% is sufficient to operate a bank, including its overhead and payroll.

Add another 1% as reserve for losses (if loans are made with business-like discretion and not racketeered) and another such factor for profit, and we find a 3% interest rate to be fully sufficient for all reasonable, decent purposes.

This would cut the approximate 50% to 60% of the rent dollar that goes to debt service to about 1/5th or 20% or, to be generous, say, 25%—savings of 35% of the rent of each and every person in this country. What a different life each of us could lead!

Again, to state it briefly, there is no doubt that the banks are not useful to the construction, maintenance or rehabilitation of housing. Rather, they are the root cause of the intolerable failure to utilize our wealth, technology, and the capabilities that could, if freed from the paralysis of this colossus, build an unimaginable wealth of housing and help to fulfill other needs of the people.

Indeed, since we pay in taxes (directly and indirectly) all the sums that the governments pay over to the banks, the speculators and the others who feed at this nourishing trough—would we not do much better to cut these interfering "experts" out (since they produce nothing) and use these vast funds to build housing—directly out of public funds, *in the public domain, without bond issue* (therefore, no interest), *under tenant controls* that start with planning and go on through administration, maintenance, rents, and amenities?

The answer must be yes! No longer can there be even the faintest hope that real estate/banking can do it for us.

But what does "public domain" mean? And just how do we get the many billions of dollars with which to build what is needed?

Chapter III

HOUSING IN THE PUBLIC DOMAIN: WHAT DOES IT MEAN?*

Over and over since the thirties the government has given lip service to the fact that it must help provide housing at low and moderate rents. But the history of government subsidies, from new construction to "rehabs," from Mitchell-Lama to Municipal Loan, from Urban Renewal to tax abatement for luxury housing, and on city, state and federal levels, has been a history of tremendous profits made by banks, bondholders, landlords, builders and speculators.

These tremendous profits come in part from the subsidies of tax money that first get the housing built, and in part from tenants' rents. Under the pressure of this economic crisis, we find government housing officials insisting that the tenants will have to bail out the moneylenders, no matter what the cost in human terms.

Housing must be by and for the people

Real estate investors have long since abdicated their responsibility to provide decent, safe and sanitary housing at rents people can afford. The property interest of real estate/banking

*This section on *Housing in the Public Domain* is based on the official statement of the Metropolitan Council on Housing adopted at its annual conference in November, 1975.

must give way to human rights. Housing must be in the Public Domain, under tenant control.

The Metropolitan Council on Housing, in calling for HOUSING IN THE PUBLIC DOMAIN UNDER TENANT CONTROL WITH DIRECT ALLOCATION OF FUNDS, seeks to develop a program and movement to meet the immediate and desperate need for decent housing. This has to be a program unlike those that have been developed before, a program which takes the profit out of housing and thus permits it to be built in vast, affordable quantities.

We do not mean to establish another bureaucracy like the New York City Housing Authority. The Housing Authority does provide relatively low-rent housing for a fraction of the New Yorkers who desperately need it, and the long waiting lists for public housing apartments are proof of the need. But the long lists are also proof of how desperate people are to get out of privately owned slums. They prefer public housing, even though public housing as we know it has many built-in drawbacks: specifically, the attitude that public housing is provided as charity rather than as a basic human right to shelter.

Nor do we mean to turn housing over to the Housing and Development Administration (HDA), New York City's housing bureaucracy or any such agency. The HDA serves the real estate industry, not the needs of tenants. Its leaders are real estate oriented. HDA's methods of financing the Mitchell-Lama and Municipal Loan Programs are proof of this real estate/banking orientation. The high rents and constant rent increases the HDA approves under these programs show its failure to administer housing at rents tenants can afford.

How would it work? A people's Housing Board and Tenant Committees

We mean to establish a Housing Board consisting of tenants, just plain people—no bureaucrats, bankers or real estate people—which would coordinate Tenant Committees. Each

Tenant Committee would be elected by a majority of all the tenants within each multiple dwelling (including three-family homes).

To set policies and to manage and coordinate housing in the people's behalf, more than anything else we need—A DECENT ATTITUDE. Given that, the rest will come. The Housing Board and Tenant Committees can learn the technicalities of financing, operations, construction and design and all else needed to build and run housing. They can hire and supervise the services of people who are bookkeepers, bricklayers, electricians, plumbers, architects and other specialists.

The Housing Board and Tenant Committees need basically to maintain the point of view of the tenant, the people who inhabit the building, those who work for a living and who should be able to come home to relax and refresh themselves instead of coming home to a depressing hassle.

What goes into Public Domain?

The following types of buildings would be the first to be declared in the public domain and would be run by Tenant Committees. These are examples and should not be considered a final list.

EXISTING HOUSING

• All residential buildings on which *taxes have not been paid for three months* (instead of the current one year the city must wait before it can begin to foreclose) shall be foreclosed by "*in rem*" proceedings and taken over by the Housing Board. The present practice of auctioning them off to new landlords shall be discontinued. Instead, they shall be renovated, repaired, refurbished and made decently liveable by the city. They shall then be declared to be in the Public Domain, made available for occupancy and run by the existing tenants (based upon the procedures and criteria outlined above and as further developed through experience).

In this time of crisis, New Yorkers must be aware that the real estate industry now owes more than $1 billion in uncollected real estate taxes and water and sewer charges, which have been paid by tenants in their rent money and never turned over to the city.

• Buildings where necessary services have seriously diminished or where the landlord has not bothered to collect rent for three months.

• Buildings where the landlord is guilty of discrimination—of any kind, especially racial discrimination—the worst kind, since it divides people against themselves and therefore leaves them open to landlord manipulation and abuse.

NEW HOUSING

New housing is to be built by direct allocation of government funds, and held and run as described below. In New York City, the Housing Board should have a goal of building at least 200,000 units per year; in the United States, at least 5 million units per year. Direct allocation of federal, state, and/or local government funds means paying for the construction in cash, out of government revenues which will have already been raised—no borrowing, no mortgages, no bond issues. Direct allocation will reduce rents by approximately 50 percent because financing—that is, the costs of borrowing money from banks or from other moneylenders through mortgages and bond issues—double the construction and operating costs of a building. There will be no real estate taxes on buildings in the Public Domain.

How will buildings in the Public Domain be run?

Buildings in the Public Domain will be run by the tenants as follows (this is an early proposal, not a final formula):

RENTS

Rents will be based on no more than 15% of income for the present. Eventually, rents will be lowered to a smaller portion of income. In any event, exceptions will be made for tenants on fixed income where the remaining 85% of income is not enough to cover other necessities of life, and for those who are unemployed and whose unemployment insurance runs out.

MANAGEMENT AND FINANCING

All operations and maintenance will be managed by a committee of tenant occupants, with the budget for maintenance set and payments authorized jointly by the Housing Board and Tenant Committee. Where major repairs are necessary, appropriations for such work will be made directly from public funds. For existing buildings coming under Public Domain, mortgages and real estate taxes will not be paid. The needs of the tenants will take priority over other liens on the buildings. As rents will not include real estate taxes, alternative methods of financing that part of the city budget now financed by real estate taxes will be obtained from the wide variety of available sources (see page 124).

OCCUPANCY, VACANCIES AND PRIORITIES

All vacancies as they occur will be filled, based on a roster of tenants who have enrolled with the Housing Board as requiring decent, safe and sanitary housing—taking into consideration current apartment conditions, the need for an apartment as close as possible to the place of work, children's schools and health facilities. Top priority will be given to emergency conditions where tenants require immediate shelter.

RENT LIMITATIONS ON PRIVATE REAL ESTATE

In buildings which are not yet taken over by the Housing Board, that is, in regular privately owned buildings, rents are to be set at no more than 15% of the income of each tenant. Where the landlord chooses not to own such a building, the building under these conditions shall be placed in the Public Domain.

Housing is a basic human right

Landlords feed on profits, but neither landlords nor profits are necessary for decent, integrated housing at rents people can afford. The government, through direct allocation of our tax dollars, spends billions on defense and wastes and tolerates the misuse of many other billions, that could instead be channeled for human needs. It already pays the costs, with our tax money, for certain needs and services such as the free use of roads and sidewalks, fire, police, sanitation and schools. There is no greater need than shelter, and we must create the mechanism within the government to meet this need.

Endless billions of dollars abound for this purpose as well as for people's other needs. We merely have to organize the sensible use of these funds. Chapter IV indicates what these sources are.

Chapter **IV**

SOURCES OF
AVAILABLE FUNDS

The responsibility is ours

It is evident by now, that landlords/bankers are not interested in building shelter for people, but rather in using housing as a means of extracting maximum profit. The results are tragic. The 13 million families who suffer serious housing deprivation cannot be permitted to become 14, 15 or 16 million in the next few years.

The problem of providing shelter for people and not for profit therefore falls upon us. We know what rents we can afford to pay in order to have enough left for food, clothing, recreation, education, medical expenses, and all else that life requires.

The machinery set up to bring this into being cannot be blueprinted in advance. It will develop through the tenants' own life experiences, through organizations such as the Metropolitan Council on Housing and through all the other forms that the good common sense of the common people will bring into being.

It has happened before in history. It will happen again. It will happen in housing because our cities are decaying before our eyes, and the billions of dollars that the government spends to alleviated the decay do not alleviate it but go right into the landlord/bankers' already swollen profits.

Defining our housing needs

Before we begin to discuss where the money comes from we should define our needs. How much housing do we need? How many dollars will that take?

Back in the 1930's, President Roosevelt spoke of "one-third of a nation ill-housed, ill-fed and ill-clothed." In terms of housing, the situation that existed then continues today and has deteriorated even further.

During the depression of the 1930's, there certainly was no building program to fulfill the nation's housing needs. During the first half of the 1940's, there was no building whatever; there was World War II. During the latter half of the 1940's, and since, the shortage has remained and has grown, despite some construction. As we indicated earlier, this shortage has been good for profits.

In the meantime, two other forces have been at work. First, since the 1930's the population has increased by 74%; and second, the existing housing has continued to deteriorate, naturally, with age, and unnaturally, with landlords' milking buildings to obtain their superprofits.

In the best boom years, the real estate industry and the government together have managed to construct not more than two million housing units per year nationally.

This, by no means, can be said to be our maximum effort. First, because we know that real estate interests deliberately have maintained a shortage; second, because in all that period we have had unemployed citizens in varying numbers who could have been employed to construct housing; and third, because we have used valuable people and materials to construct office buildings that are now a glut on the market and where foreclosures are taking place at a rate that gladdens the heart of the banker and mortgagee in their search for good things at bargain rates for the future.

Especially because today 7½ million people are unemployed throughout the nation, it is possible, indeed necessary, to put forth a perspective of building at least five million housing units per year. This program must go on until there is enough housing built for everyone in need of shelter, and then we must tear down and replace all the existing dilapidated, unsafe, unsanitary and overcrowded housing that disgraces our wealthy nation.

Of these five million units, New York City will require not less than 200,000 units per year, since we lead the nation in decay, in slums, in degradation *and* in high rents.

How much will it cost?

It is estimated that the cost of constructing a unit of housing (an apartment) in New York City is in the area of $40,000. Much of this figure is due—aside from debt-service payments—to land speculation, among other things, and, as recognized by the United Nations "Habitat" Conference, there must be devices for stopping, as well as recapturing, this speculation.

By the simple device of having all housing built by *direct allocation of tax funds* (federal, state and city), the 50% to 60% of construction and operations/finance costs that come from the payment of debt service, and which are now the major items of expense, can be eliminated.

By this we mean that the government shall not issue bonds to provide the capital for housing. Therefore, there will be no interest to pay; there will be no mortgage to repay and, of course, no profits to the landlord, banker, bondholder or mortgagee.

As a consequence, the $40,000 per unit cost of construction will be cut by more than half. There will be no debt service. Thus, the cost per unit—all else aside for the moment—will become $20,000. (Rents, too, will fall in the same proportion.) So, five million units multiplied by $20,000 per unit is $100 billion.

The Pentagon budget alone for the 1976-77 fiscal year is about $113 billion. And that budget is not financed by bonds. It comes from the direct allocation of our tax dollars!

So it should not be too difficult to imagine how a $100 billion housing program—in the Public Domain—could be financed.

But the Pentagon is only one source. We are not advocating total elimination of the defense budget. We merely want to reduce the amount of "overkill" by trimming off some of its fat, waste and corruption. There are hundreds, if not thousands, of other sources of funds for housing and people's other needs in our bloated economy.

Budget of available funds

As an examination of the budget will show, the amount of funds available for housing—construction, rehabilitation and maintenance—as well as people's other needs, is truly astronomical.

The available funds are divided into six categories for simplicity, but also to permit the reader to separate and eliminate any item or category which in his/her opinion is not practical.

In examining this budget these facts should be borne in mind: Many items are referred to, but no money figure is attached to them, since they are imponderables. In many cases, the figures are much too conservative because, for example, projecting New York State or New York City figures nationally would have been utter guesswork, and compiling accurate figures would have been a huge research project far beyond the necessities of this study. Figures on corporate tax avoidance are limited merely to those few cited and are by no means a roster of corporate chiseling. Finally, in citing figures such as Secretary of the Treasury Simon's approximation of the amount of tax loopholes that exist in our laws, we have deliberately selected the lowest attribution. Many authorities have advanced figures two, three or more times as large. The same is true of the cost of the Vietnam War, for example.

The categories into which we have placed items in our Budget of Available Funds are:

Budget categories

1 *Identifiable, realistic amounts that can be saved.*
2 *In some cases, where amounts are regional or not specific, we*

project low and conservative figures for the nation as a whole or for the particular entity.

3 *Savings resulting from the reduction of interest rates to a practical and economically viable 3% per year.*

4 *Recapture of overspeculated land and real estate values and the inflation-causing corporate profit spree.*

5 *Wealth created by putting the unemployed to work.*

6 *Wasted funds–actually expended or in planning stages–that cannot easily be recaptured, but which indicate that funds can be raised where there is a desire to do so.*

Note:

a) The category numbers above will be found attached to the item of source material from which they are derived. Source items without category numbers represent amounts too complex to compute.

b) The total Budget of Available Funds is organized by category, commencing at page 118.

The financial economic framework

The size and scope of our enormous and wasteful economy must be comprehended in order to understand how our program fits into it and how the funds to finance Housing in the Public Domain can be extracted from it.

Land and structure speculation

Here are some of the more important elements of the financial/economic framework in which we, as a nation, live, work and pay tribute.

Category #

4 Total value of real estate, land and structures in the United States, in 1971 was estimated to be worth $3.5 trillion (3,500 billion dollars).

(Harry A. Golemon, ed., *Financing Real Estate Development*)

The annual gain is at the level of approximately $200 billion per year, with the dominant proportion represented by increments in structure value. Total value has been rising at an average annual rate of 7% from 1968-1971.

(Harry A. Golemon, ed., *Financing Real Estate Development*)

The erudite words above mean, in more simple language, that speculation has raised the "values" of land and structures by 7% per year. Without factual knowledge of what the rate of speculative rise was in the previous three years, let us presume as one possibility that the same rate applied.

Therefore, if, as the United Nations "Habitat" Conference decided was necessary in many cases, we were to recapture this speculative increase for those 7 years (see bracketed section below), in simple arithmetic it would amount to 49%. However, since the rise is compounded, it is well over 50%.

> In the absence of precise facts regarding the rate of the speculative rise in real estate "values" prior to 1968, it is perhaps an exaggeration to apply the 7% rate to those years. To be carefully conservative, let us cut that rate in half—3½%. Thus we extend the time period from 7 years to 10 years in order to reach the same 50% level of real estate speculative inflation.

Limiting ourselves to either period of time—that is, either the 7 or the 10 years prior to 1971—and again limiting ourselves to 50% (the rate without compounding), the recapture of only these few years of inflation-causing speculation would make available for the purpose of housing and other needs of the people, the incredible sum of $1.75 trillion ($1,750 billion).

Note: *It is worth underscoring that this basic and most valuable of all properties increased at the astonishing rate of 50%; that is, in 7 or 10 years the "value" of U.S. real estate increased by half again the "values" that had been built up in the previous nearly 200 years of the life of our nation.* Can one wonder any more about what causes inflation?

Federal level sources

DEBT AND COSTS

Category #
3   The total net debt of government and private sectors in 1975 was 3 trillion dollars.

(If we take 6% as a "guesstimate" of the average interest rate—remember the MAC bonds were up to 11%—the amount paid to the banks, bondholders and the upper-crust generally, as interest, would be $180 billion annually.)

Of this $3 trillion, the federal, state and local governments owed $1 trillion 187 billion. The balance presumably was private industry's.

(U.S. Commerce Department via United
Press International report, published
in *Providence Journal,* June 10, 1976)

The House of Representatives voted to raise the national public debt limit from $627 billion to $700 billion.

(*New York Times,* June 15, 1976)

Interest on the public debt paid by the federal government in 1975 was $32.7 billion.

(*U.S. Budget,* Fiscal 1977)

The public debt is *never* repaid. We have never, since our founding, been without debt. On the contrary, it always goes higher!

THE ECONOMY AND THE BUDGET

Category #
       The Gross National Product for
              1974 was: $1 trillion 397 billion
              1975 estimated $1 trillion 474 billion
              1976 projected $1 trillion 651 billion
                             (*New York Times,* December 1, 1975)

The United States Budget for fiscal 1976 is $408.4 billion.
(U.S. Budget, Office of Management and Budget)

Of the total Federal budget, 34% goes to "national defense."
(1975 *U.S. Statistical Abstract*)

Of five million Federal employees, 3.2 million work for the Defense Department.
(New York Times, June 19, 1976)

DEFENSE, FOREIGN AID AND SPACE PROGRAMS

Category #

1   For fiscal 1976, the Defense Budget was $104.7 billion. With additional appropriations, it was later stated to be $113 billion.
(New York Times, June 17, 1976)

6   The authorization for the production of the B-1 supersonic bomber was $21.4 billion. (Note: unofficial estimated total cost is $100 billion.)
(Department of Defense, *Selected Acquisition Report*, December 31, 1975)

6   The Air Force is developing an Intercontinental Ballistic Missile that may cost $30 billion.
(New York Times, October 10, 1976)

1   Earmarked (in the Defense Budget) for National Intelligence, $4 billion. (Remember the recent FBI and CIA scandals?)
(New York Times, November 19, 1975)

6   Officially estimated cost of the Vietnam War to 1973, $111.6 billion. (Ultimate cost, unknown.) Unofficially, the cost estimates vary from $150 to $300 billion.
(U.S. Budget, Fiscal 1977)

1   Estimated total Foreign Aid, 1976, $6.6 billion, of which military portion is $2.0 billion.
(U.S.Budget, Fiscal 1977)

1   Portion of budget marked for "International Affairs," $4.6 billion.
(U.S. Budget, Fiscal 1977)

6   United States Space Program, total outlay
         1960—1975 $78.6 billion
1   1975 alone $ 4.9 billion
                                    (1975 *Statistical Abstract*)

TAXES–WHO PAYS THEM AND WHO DOES NOT

Category #
1   Over the years, there has been a decided shift of the tax
         burden away from the corporations and onto the shoulders
         of the individual taxpayer.

                              Percentage of tax burden
         Major sources   *Year* 1967 1970 1974 1975 (*est.*)

         Individual income taxes   41.1 46.7 44.9   43.6

         Corporation income taxes   22.7 16.9 14.6   14.5
                    (Congressman Charles Vanik (Demo-
                    crat—Ohio) in his 4th annual report to
                    Congress. Reported in *Economic Notes*,
                    Labor Research Association, September
                    1976)

1   Treasury Secretary William Simon stated that the elimina-
         tion of all but standard income tax deductions, would in-
         crease U.S. tax income by $50 billion.
                              (*New York Times*, December 4, 1975)

1   In 1974, 244 persons with incomes in excess of $200,000 paid
         no Federal income tax. Five of this group had incomes in
         excess of $1 million.
                                   (*New York Times*, May 8, 1976)

         Vice President Nelson Rockefeller paid *no* Federal income
         tax in 1971.
                                  (*New York Times*, May 16, 1976)

         Ronald Reagan paid *no* California income tax in 1970, and
         most likely no Federal income tax in 1970.
                                  (*New York Times*, May 16, 1976)

         Anthony L. Conrad, President of RCA Corporation, did not

file income tax returns, nor pay any income taxes for five years.

(New York Times, September 17, 1976)

6   The Tax Reform Bill of 1976 attempted to reduce the income tax rates for the top 1% of the richest Americans from 70% down to 50%. This would have affected the 250,000 wealthiest people.

There are 180,000 millionaires in the United States, according to the Internal Revenue Service; 90,836 were women and 89,164, men.

(The International Teamster, February 1976)

RIP-OFF UNDER THE GUISE OF HOUSING

Category #
1   *Federal New Towns Program*
The United States Department of Housing and Urban Development (HUD) is re-evaluating its "new-town" program under which the federal government has guaranteed $280 million in loans since 1970.

At the time of the publication of the article, $21 million in loan guarantees for one project—Gananda, outside Rochester, New York—has been written off as a total loss.

For eleven of the projects, HUD has been picking up the interest payments on the bonds since July 1st.

The total interest burden on all the bonds amounts to about $20 million a year.

As of the end of March, the Government had paid out $11 million in interest.

(New York Times, July 23, 1976)

2   *Federal Section 235 (Home Ownership Program)*
Almost $2.5 billion was pumped into housing by HUD in 1971, a large portion of which went into the 235 program which was designed to *help some families buy homes with very little cash,* reducing interest rates to as low as 5%—the banks getting the difference between that and the market rate.

"With amazing candor, Secretary of HUD, Carla Hills

stated that the main goal of the program is to stimulate the construction industry, *improving the housing of the millions who now live in squalor would be secondary.*" (Emphasis added.)

(*The Real Problem is Poverty*, by Representative John Conyers, Jr., in *The Nation*, January 24, 1976)

In Detroit, the default rate on Section 235 homes reached 30%. This has occurred in many other parts of the nation also, including Jamaica, New York.

FEDERAL MISCELLANY–AN EXAMPLE

Category #
6   The billions wasted on the Law Enforcement Assistance Administration "should have been spent instead on abolishing slums and eliminating racism," stated an editorial in the Madison, Wisconsin *Capital-Times*, declaring that that agency is "beyond repair." In its eight-year existence, it wasted $4 billion.

(*Daily World*, September 16, 1976)

Private industry sources: corporate profits

American Telephone and Telegraph Company recorded profits at an all-time high for the third quarter of 1976, $1.01 billion. (This figure represents an all-time record high for any company for any quarter year.)

(*New York Times*, September 20, 1976)

Corporate Earnings—first quarter of 1976

Company	Jan. Feb. Mar. earnings	Percentage change from 1975 (same quarter)
Amerada Hess	$ 44,200,000	+ 60.1%
Delta Airlines	11,500,000	+ 173.8%
Martin Marietta	9,400,000	+ 168.6%
Honeywell	13,600,000	+1136.4%

Category #

R.C.A.	34,300,000	+ 101.8%
General Motors	800,000,000	+1255.9%
Du Pont	137,500,000	+ 545.5%

(New York Times, April 15, 20, 23 and 29, 1976)

Corporate profits surged 44% in the first quarter of 1976 over the previous year.

(New York Times, May 8, 1976)

4   *After-tax* corporate profits in the second quarter of 1976 were at the seasonally adjusted annual rate of $82.7 billion.

(New York Times, September 21, 1976)

Six sugar refiners were indicted by a United States jury for price-fixing.

•Sucrest Corporation and United States Sugar declared extra dividends.

(New York Times, December 20, 1974)

•Great Western, the largest sugar processor in the country, reported a 1,200% jump in after-tax profits in the third quarter of 1974.

(Daily World, November 8, 1974)

Congressman Vanik (Democrat-Ohio) in submitting his fourth annual tax report to Congress, noted the following three facts:

1   *•The average tax rate paid by most big businesses in 1974—was 22.6%. The rate mandated by law is 48%—more than twice as high!*

4   •In 1974 there were eight companies (in that study) that paid *no* Federal Corporate Income Taxes, although they had combined profts of $843,974,000.

•These companies are:
  Ford Motor Company
  Lockheed Aircraft
  Honeywell
  United States Industries
  American Airlines
  Eastern Airlines
  American Electric Power Company
  Allstate Insurance Company

Category #
4   18 companies in 1974 paid an effective United States Income
        Tax rate of 10% *or less.* They paid $270,430,000 in taxes on
        profits of $5,322,683,000. That average income tax rate
        equals 5%:

                •These companies are: *Effective*
                                                                Rate
Consolidated Edison Company of New York   less than 1%
Occidental Petroleum Corporation   1.6%
Chase Manhattan Corporation   2.9%
Texaco, Inc.   3.3%
Bankers Trust New York Corporation   4.8%
Northwest Airlines   5.2%
Mobil Oil Corporation   5.3%
Texas Gulf   6.1%
Pennzoil Company   7.1%
BankAmerica Corporation   9.9%
Commonwealth Edison Company   10.0%

                              (*Economic Notes,* Labor Research
                              Association, September, 1976)

Just what profits corporate industry wants can be judged
from the following statement of Pierre A. Rinfret, president
of Rinfret Associates, an economic advisory firm (whose
views, in this respect, are similar to those of Citibank).

"There is not enough physical capacity to put everybody
to work," he said. "*Less real money is being invested in new
plants and equipment today than in 1969. Profits have not
been there for capital investments. Profits are inadequate by
any measure.*" (Emphasis added.)

                              (*New York Times,* August 4, 1976)

But—the people, how are they doing?

1976 consumer prices were projected to be 172% of 1967
prices.

                              (*New York Times,* December 1, 1975)

Category #

1   The Federal Trade Commission estimated that of total consumer purchases of $900 billion, fraudulent practices have bilked consumers of $80—$100 billion.

> (*New York Times*, August 22, 1975,
> "Op Ed" article by I. Philip Sipser)

25,880,000 Americans subsisted below the poverty line in 1975—an increase over 1974 of 2,500,000 people, the largest increase in one year since 1959. (The poverty level for a non-farm family was $5,500 per year.)

> (United Press International dispatch
> published in *Daily World*, September 30, 1976)

Between August of 1971 and July of 1974, the *average weekly earnings* of workers rose from $128.02 per week to $154.90 per week. However, *real weekly earnings*–after adjustment for inflation—during this period were $92.62 which *dropped* to $91.04 in July, 1974.

> (United States Bureau of Labor Statistics
> published in *New York Times*, September 11, 1974)

Unemployment nationally was at the rate of 7.9% in August, 1976, and totalled 7,506,000 people.

> (United States Bureau of Labor Statistics
> published in *Daily World*, September 4, 1976)

George Meany, President of the AFL-CIO, has estimated unemployment at 10.5%, if those too discouraged to look for work are included.

In the New York metropolitan area, the unemployment rate is 9.8%, or 25% higher than the national average.

> (United States Department of Labor published
> in *New York Times*, September 4, 1976)

Among Black, Latin and minority people, the rate of unemployment is variously stated to be as high as 20% to 25%.

Among youth, aged 16 to 19, the U.S. Bureau of Labor Statistics found unemployment in June 1977 in New York City, to be the highest among eleven major American cities. White youths, unemployed, constituted 74%. Black and other minorities youth constituted 86%. The national averages were 42.1% for whites and 66.3% for minorities.

> (*New York Times*, August 2, 1977)

New York State level sources

Category #

"Where can your corporation taxes be nearly $00.00? *In New York State.* Where, for new and expanded plants, you can receive business tax credits of nearly 100%."
(Excerpted from an advertisement of the
New York State Department of Commerce
published in *New York Times*, December 15, 1974)

1   Many $30,000 State jobs are called part-time jobs by a special board set up by Governor Carey. Some need only work a few hours per week.
(New York Times, September 5, 1976)

1   New York State can save $4.2 million a year by moving its offices from the World Trade Center, says the State's Office of General Services.
(New York Times, June 7, 1976)

1   New York State legislators voted themselves an extra $880,000 in "lulus" (in lieu of expenses).
(New York Times, June 3, 1976)

1   New York State agencies keep large non-interest bearing accounts at favored banks, such as:
• New York State Department of Taxation and Finance had on deposit with Bankers Trust Company, $11 million. (James G. Hellmuth, Republican Party State Treasurer, is Vice President of Bankers Trust Company.)
• The State Lottery opened a $4 million account at a Bankers Trust subsidiary in Albany.
(New York Times, January 5, 1976)

6   The New York State Mall in Albany cost $985 million. The original estimate was $250 million.

The banks and other giants

Category #

1   The Legislature of the State of New York decided it was time to make the banks pay a bit of their fair share of taxes. So they raised the banks' taxes from 8% ot 12% (with a 30% sur-

Category #

charge only for the years 1975 and 1976). This was to have brought in $275 million. Instead, it yielded $190.9 million—30% short. Why?

According to John G. Heimann, then the State's Superintendant of Banks, the banks reduced their tax rate by *siphoning off income* and *channeling it into reserve funds* set aside for losses from bad loans.

(*New York Times,* May 5, 1976)

1   The New York Telephone Company and its parent company, American Telephone and Telegraph, are using an ancient loophole to avoid paying state taxes on over $1 billion of revenue. The loophole law goes back to the 19th century, which rules out taxing income attributable to interstate operations.

(*New York Post,* October 15, 1976)

1   A 1% tax on the income-yielding assets (such as stocks, bonds, mortgages, loans, etc.) of banks, insurance companies and related financial institutions in the State of New York, would yield from $2 billion to $4 billion per year. (This tax would be limited to the income derived from the State of New York only.)

(Proposal by New York State
Assemblyman Frank J. Barbaro,
November 12, 1975)

4   New York State built and paid for production facilities for the Consolidated Edison Company of New York that cost $500 million and gave these facilities to the company *free.*
(Jack Newfield, *Village Voice,*
April 26, 1976)

Richard Ravitch, head of HRH Construction Company, and builder of the floundering $95 million Manhattan Plaza, was appointed by Governor Carey as the first Executive Director of the Emergency Financial Control Board, the State's watch-dog over the City's watch-dog, the Municipal Assistance Corporation. Both are banker dominated. Ravitch was also Chairman of the floundering-foundering Urban Development Corporation.

(*New York Post,* October 14, 1975)

Another state–Arizona

Category #

No attempt is being made to gather even a minor part of the available evidence that indicates the corruption and other forms of wasted money that can be used for our Budget of Available Funds. As a token, we offer this bit of Americana from Arizona:

4   The Attorney General of the State of Arizona "estimated that the sale of virtually worthless land mortgages have bilked investors of $500 million during the last decade."

(New York Times, October 5, 1976)

As to its part in the budget: Should it be multiplied by 49 states (since New York State is well represented)? Or by 149 or 1049?

Tempting as this is as an extension of reality to the rest of the country, there is in the very partial evidence we put forth in this document so vastly much more than is needed to fulfill our budget that the temptation is easily brushed aside.

So this is our token. Use your imagination and your own multiplier.

New York City level sources

MUNICIPAL MISBEHAVIOR
Category #

The 1976-77 budget for New York City was $12.5 billion.

(New York Times, April 15, 1976)

3   The debt service in the 1976-77 budget was $2.3 billion.

(New York Times, April 15, 1976)

(Note: Debt service is a euphemism for the payment of interest to the banks. When principal is repaid, it is again re-borrowed. This is called "roll-over." The city's debt never decreases. It always grows larger.)

As a percentage of the budget, debt service is 19%. (Almost one cent out of every five cents of our total taxes goes to the banks and bondholders.)

(New York Times, April 15, 1976)

Category #

In July, 1974, Comptroller Harrison Goldin rejected as "unconscionable" a bid for New York City notes by the usual consortium of banks at the rate of 7.92%.

• One week later, he borrowed from these same sources $800 million short-term funds at 8.586%.

• On November 4, 1974, he borrowed $150 million tax-anticipation notes at 8.34%.

• On December 2, 1974, he again borrowed $600 million in one-year notes at 9.479%.

• On November 22, 1974, Mayor Beame announced a deficit of $400 million, of which *$104 million was debt-service cost overrun.* (In plain English, this means the extra high interest rates which the banks demanded and got, while forcing the city to "economize" by firing thousands of workers.)

(Study prepared by Martin Rosenblatt, a member of the Social Service Employees Union, Local 371, as published in the *Daily World*, March 21, 1975)

The annual debt service of New York City increased 157% in two decades and mainly reflects past borrowings.

(Professor Donald Haider and Thomas H. Elmore, as published in the *New York Times*, March 30, 1975)

Federal guarantees of up to $7 billion were voted to cover New York City debts.

(New York Times, November 1, 1975)

(Note: Even though these bonds and notes are now federally guaranteed, and thus loss-proof, the interest rates— tax-exempt—have not come down.)

Matthew J. Troy, Jr., New York City Councilman and Chairman of the Council's Finance Committee, pleaded guilty to charges of filing a false income tax return. He received a two-month jail sentence and a fine of $5,000. He agreed to make restitution of $37,000 he had taken from the estates of law clients.

(New York Times, September 30, 1976)

"HOW NEW YORK BECAME A FISCAL JUNKIE. ON THE PATH TO DEBT ADDICTION, THERE WERE

THE EXPENSE FIX, THE REVENUE FIX, THE CAPI-
TAL FIX AND THE OUTRIGHT DEFICIT FIX."
(Title of an article by Steven R. Weisman in the
New York Times, Magazine Section, August 17, 1975)

*WHILE DETERIORATION SPREADS AND BANKRUPTCY
THREATENS, OUR CITY FATHERS CONTINUE
ON THEIR IRRESPONSIBLE COURSE*

Category #

In the face of a glut in the commercial and industrial real
estate market, to the point where there is a high degree of
bankruptcy and foreclosure proceedings among and against
the owners, the Committee Chairman of the New York City
Council stated that a measure (requested by the Beame
Administration) would be passed within two weeks that
would exempt from real estate taxation for periods from 10 to
19 years, new and reconstructed commercial and industrial
buildings.

(New York Times, September 30, 1976)
(See page 44, Local Law 58.)

1   The Municipal Loan Program
This is a scandal-ridden giveaway to real estate
sharpshooters. It was temporarily closed down in 1971 by
Mayor Lindsay and *one* public official went to jail. Foreclosure actions are pending against 150 of the 220 post-1967
projects. The city has already acknowledged a capital loss of
$40 million, which is expected to rise to $70 million.

(New York Times, April 2, 1976)

REAL ESTATE TAXES

Category #

1   Real Estate Taxes as a percentage of the New York City
Budget
1915—78%
1925—79%
1955—47%
1965—37%
1968—36%
1974—23%

(Public Employees Press, June 20, 1975)

Category #

1   Tax delinquencies were $1.3 billion as of January, 1976.
        (Tax Guardian, Spring, 1976)
        (Note: This is a real estate industry propaganda sheet.)

    Tax delinquencies were $1 billion by the end of 1975.
        (Letter of Reuben Klein, President of
        the New York Realty Owners Association
        as published in the *New York Post)*
    Take your choice!

1    $20 million in real estate tax assessment reductions were
    given, among others, to:
        • New York Telephone Company at 1091
    Avenue of the Americas (William Ellinghaus,
    its President, was also Chairman of the
    Municipal Assistance Corporation). $1.25 million
        • Also, on other New York
    Telephone properties $227,000
        • Rockefeller Center $9.15 million
        • Avis Corporation (on 5 buildings) $6.8 million
        • First National City Bank $1.1 million
        • Bank of New York $1.0 million
                        (City Record, as published in the
                        Daily World, August 16, 1975)

    Helmsley-Spear, one of the largest real estate outfits in the
    city, decided to stop paying real estate taxes on 190 of the
    firm's 400 residential buildings in New York City.
                        (New York Magazine, April 14, 1975)

    Borough President Robert Abrams of the Bronx stated that
    the 10 largest tax delinquents included the following:

        • The New York Bank for Savings, which failed to pay off a
    $450,000 tax bill on property it foreclosed last year.
        • The Hilton Hotel chain, which owes the city almost $2
    million in back taxes on the New Yorker Hotel.
        • A 16-story office building at Fifth Avenue and 33rd
    Street.
        • A 20-story apartment house on East 58th Street.
        • The Hotel Taft, on Seventh Avenue and 51st Street.
                        (New York Post, September 29, 1975)

Felix G. Rohatyn, Chairman of the Municipal Assistance Corporation, proposed that a stretch-out program for longer term city bonds "would permit as much as *a 20% lowering of the real estate tax."*(Emphasis added.)

(*New York Times*, September 22, 1976)

MORE GIVEAWAYS–PLANNED AND ALREADY GIVEN

Category #

1   The city is planning to sell $900 million worth of mortgages on 122 Mitchell-Lama houses with 42,000 tenants. It expects to realize only $600 million or $700 million on this sale.

(*New York Times*, August 31, 1975)

Note:

1) This turns over city-subsidized middle-income houses to real estate/banking.

2) It loses $200 to $300 million in the process.

3) Rents in these developments, already zooming, will then skyrocket!

6   New York City Third Water Tunnel—budgeted and contracted out at $100 million, revised to $384 million—a cost "overrun" of $284 million.

(*New York Times*, November 10, 1974)

1   An audit by City Comptroller Harrison Goldin says the city loses $2 million a year in Department of Parks concessions.

(*New York Times*, June 11, 1976)

6   Yankee Stadium, rebuilt by New York City money, was originally estimated to cost $24 million, will now cost $96 million.

(*New York Times*, March 16, 1976)

2   The Commodore Hotel will be rebuilt by the Trump Organization under an arrangement that will mean a loss of more than $100 million in tax revenues, through tax relief to the developer.

(*New York Times*, March 16, 1976)

The Bronx Terminal Market was leased to a private company for 99 years at a rental that is a fraction of the amount being received by the developer for its use.

(*New York Times*, March 16, 1976)

Category #

1 New York City Councilman Robert F. Wagner, Jr., stated after a ten-month study that New York City was spending $155 million a year to lease more office space than was needed.

• Major political contributors hold many of the city leases.

• In Manhattan alone, city rental payments in one year cover the full purchase price of six leased buildings.

• Councilman Wagner listed 19 lessors of property to the City who had contributed a total of $55,450 to Mayor Beame's 1973 mayoralty campaign.

(New York Times, June 26, 1976)

LANDLORDS' THREATS–CITY'S ENTICEMENTS

Category #

"In what may be a major showdown with the Beame Administration, almost all of the 1,200 owners at a mass meeting last week *voted to withhold real estate taxes, water charges, city sales taxes and major capital improvements* 'until we get relief '."

"The meeting was sponsored by the Community Housing Improvement Program (CHIP) at a seminar on the new rent law" . . . "was what CHIP termed a 'Landlord's Conservation Program'." *(Emphasis added.)*

(Real Estate Weekly, August 1, 1974)

1 To encourage and entice landlords to pay their taxes, New York City passed a law granting them an 8% discount to prepay their taxes.

(New York Times, October 5, 1975)

The ordinary citizen is not "enticed," but sent to jail if he or she evades taxes.

TAX-EXEMPT PROPERTIES

Category #

The assessed value of New York City real estate is about $60 billion.

Category #

However, there are $22 billion of tax-exempt properties:
82% of this is government-owned
18% is nongovernmental.

1   Among this 18% are included such shining gems as:
• Chrysler Building, owned by Goldman and Di Lorenzo.
• The World Trade Center—a high-rent, high-profit en-
terprise.
• Educational, religious and hospital properties that go
beyond their immediate professional needs.

1   All privately owned real estate is in large part tax-exempt,
since it pays taxes on about 50% to 60% of its real value. If
real estate were taxed on its full value (single- and two-family
homes exempted), it would yield about $1.5 billion of addi-
tional taxes.

NEW YORK CITY SUBSIDIZED HOUSING–ASSISTANCE
TO THE RICH AND TO REAL ESTATE

McKinsey and Company, a research and consulting firm,
charged that the program (New York City housing subsidy
program) is a "random approach to subsidizing upper-
income households." It further charges that 38% of the
apartments aided by tax exemption are expected to have
monthly rents of $140 or more a room, requiring a family
income of more than $30,000 a year to afford a two-bedroom
unit. Peter D. Joseph, the city's Deputy Commissioner for
Housing Production, acknowledged that most tf the buildings built in Manhattan under the program were in the
luxury-rent class. Indeed, a tax abatement building at Park
Avenue and 79th Street has one-bedroom apartments
priced at more than $1,000 a month, according to Mr.
Joseph's aides.

(*New York Times*, March 19, 1974)

A 24-story building, which two years ago was shattered by a
vast explosion, is being converted into a *luxury* apartment
tower under the city's J-51 Program. Rents will range from
$400 to $2,000 per month.

Rockrose (the landlord company) is likewise converting a

building on Broadway and 11th Street and the Hotel Albert on University Place and ten other buildings containing 1,400 units.

Taxes will be abated for periods up to 20 years.

(New York Times, August 15, 1976)

Swartzman-Litwin are building a 35-story luxury apartment building on York Avenue between 73rd and 74th Streets in Manhattan. They have put up 30 more luxury buildings on the East Side, renting from $500 to $600 per month for a one-bedroom apartment. They operate under the beneficence of New York City's J-51 Program and New York State's Section 421. Both are tax abatement programs. Swartzman-Litwin say these programs are "very enlightened."

(New York Times, May 30, 1976)

The Reynes group is converting the 21 stories and penthouse (of a commercial building at 315 Seventh Avenue) into 98 studio and one-bedroom apartments, which will rent in the high $300's to $400's range. Mr. Reynes said: *"Conversions* (under J-51) *are the only game in construction now."* *(Emphasis added.)*

(New York Times, February 25, 1976)

"A recent change in the city's J-51 tax-abatement program makes it possible for a builder to recoup approximately 60% of his investment through real estate tax reductions, and this has sparked investor interest."

(New York Times, February 14, 1976)

IF IT IS SUPPOSED TO BE GOOD FOR
THE PEOPLE, THERE IS ALWAYS AN ANGLE

Category #

Medicare-Medicaid

Federal District Judge Charles L. Brieaut, Jr., in sentencing a chiropractor to prison on 14 counts of Medicaid fraud, stated ". . . those greater minds than ours who contrived this Medicaid legislation, created a very easy and obvious means to steal public funds. Why did they do this?"

(New York Times, September 30, 1976)

Category #

22 other defendants received sentences ranging from proba-
tion to one year in prison for bilking Medicaid of more than
$600,000.

(New York Times, September 30, 1976)

2   The Medicaid Task Force of the National Governors' Conference called for the regulation, as a public utility, of the
$17 billion Medicaid program, which is scandal-ridden and
near bankruptcy.

(New York Times, September 23, 1976)

U.S. Senator Moss, referring to Medicaid mills, stated that
the city alone lost $340 million through fraud and abuse in
this program.

(New York Times, September 23, 1976)

Costs of Medicaid are rising 50% faster than the Consumers
Price Index.

(New York Times, September 23, 1976)

New York officials place Medicaid frauds at 20%.

(New York Times, August 31, 1976)

Day-care centers

1   Day-care centers are one of the biggest giveaways in the
city. The city is committed to pay a total of $300 million over
the lease periods up to 10 years for the 170 centers that it
directly leases.

(New York Times, May 4, 1976)

Six groups of day-care center operators own 69 centers.
Over the 15- and 20-year terms of the leases, these groups
will collect $129 million from the City of New York, which
also pays the real estate taxes and maintenance.

(New York Times, September 14, 1976)

Akiba Ehrenfeld, who owns seven centers and will collect
$18 million from the city, and more than $1 million in 1974
alone, reported on his federal income tax an adjusted gross
income of $4,500.

(New York Times, September 14, 1976)

"Among the beneficiaries of the day-care leases were former
Brooklyn Assemblyman Leonard Simon; Brooklyn Coun-

Category #

cilman Sam Wright; Stanley Lowell, who was one of Bernard Bergman's lawyers; the late Sidney Ungar, a notorious slumlord; and N. Hilton Rosen, whose brother, Richard Rosen, was a commissioner in the Lindsay administration, and whose wife was a City Council member."

(Village Voice, September 27, 1976)

Free school lunch program

1 The free school-lunch program, which in New York State is expected to cost $63 million to $73 million, was charged by the Department of Agriculture as "heavily plagued by mismanagement by the state, waste and theft at some food distribution sites and profiteering and contract violations by a member of food distributing organizations."

(New York Times, September 24, 1976)

"But the school board's investigation found that during the period examined—from October 1974 to March 1976—a total of 54 large orders, each in excess of $5,000, and with a combined value of $2.2 million, were split into 728 'open market' orders. Each open-market order came to less than $5,000 and thus was not subject to the usual competitive bidding required of large orders."

(New York Times, September 2, 1976)

Nursing homes

2 New York State Attorney General Louis Lefkowitz stated that one nursing home owner, Eugene Hollander, had defrauded the state of $6.3 million in Medicaid.

(New York Times, July 30, 1976)

Nursing-home owner Eugene Hollander submitted a bill to Medicaid for $360,000, which he called "patient-related expenses" but were for personal expenses, such as $10,000 of personal furniture, $54,000 for two Renoir paintings and another $16,700 for a painting by Maurice Utrillo.

(New York Times, February 3, 1976)

One nursing home, the Park Crescent in New York City, owned by the notorious Bernard Bergman, inflated construction costs of the home by $2.4 million, and charged this sum to Medicaid.

(New York Times, June 19, 1976)

Category #

It was found that the same home had been milked of more than $1 million by withholding payments for mortgage interest, taxes, pension contribution, fuel and milk, while receiving these funds from Medicaid.

(New York Times, June 19, 1976)

The same Bernard Bergman received a four-month jail sentence.

(New York Times, June 18, 1976)

Al Schwartz, an Assistant Health Commissioner who was accused of "coziness" with nursing-home operators, was appointed to supervise Medicaid and methadone clinics in New York City.

(New York Times, March 28, 1976)

Charles J. Hynes, the Special State Prosecutor for nursing homes, said that in the second year of his investigation, he would uncover at least $70 million of Medicaid overcharges. Among these overcharges were bills for personal maids, private residential landscaping, personal travel, personal food at phenomenal levels, personal luggage, works of art, vast quantities of liquor, interior decorating expenses, personal dental and medical care, heating fuel for private residences, personal charitable contributions, profits to investors, vacation expenses, private real estate taxes, private automobiles, mink coats, personal investment stocks, personal servants, entertainment, legal fees, theater tickets, stereo equipment, and extensive secret personal profits.

(New York Times, January 11, 1976)

The unemployed: a source of vast wealth

Our press, our economists and our government officials constantly decry the drain on our economic resources caused by the unemployed. They cite the depletion of the Unemployment Reserve Funds and the mounting costs of welfare. Actually, they are standing on their heads and see the world upside down.

There is no wealth without workers. Gold in the mine is

Category #

wealth only when extracted and refined by workers. So with coal and other minerals. Automobiles and refrigerators are useful and are sources of wealth only when the components are manufactured and assembled by workers. Wheat and cauliflower are useful as foods only when first planted by farm-workers and processed and packaged and transported by workers. So to keep workers unemployed is not only a waste of human beings, but also a waste of great potential wealth.

Our standing-on-the-heads economists tell us that if we do not have unemployed, we will have inflation. This is patent nonsense. There are numerous factors that make for inflation, but employment, even full employment, is not one of the causes. Cars, food, clothing and the other necessities of life have been priced so high that people must cut down on the consumption of these commodities. Rents have been raised far beyond a level the average person can afford. These and other high prices create the enormous profit that the huge corporations and real estate/banking interests siphon off our economy. This indefensible amount of profit is the real and major cause of inflation. If prices and profits are brought down and held down, full employment will only enrich the economy; it cannot conceivably hurt it.

With this in mind, let us examine how much wealth can be created by putting our unemployed to work:

FUNDS AVAILABLE FOR HOUSING AND OTHER
NEEDS, BY PUTTING THE UNEMPLOYED TO WORK

7.5 million people are unemployed in the United States.
(*New York Times*, September 4, 1976)

Category #

The average weekly wage of production non-supervisory workers on private non-agricultural payrolls is $175.69 per week.

(U.S. Bureau of Labor Statistics, *Employment and Earnings*, Vol. 22, No. 12, June, 1976)

7.5 million unemployed x $175 per week = approximately $1.312 billion per week.

$1.312 billion x 50 weeks per year means a national added wealth of $65.625 billion per year.

However, every dollar of payroll as it goes through the economy (the grocer, the wholesaler, the manufacturer, the builder, the bank, etc.), multiplies itself by a factor of 6.

5   Therefore, $65.625 billion of payroll x 6 = $393.75 billion *of additional wealth per year, created by putting the unemployed to useful work!*

This of itself is sufficient to solve practically all the social needs of the people of this nation, and to move us to new and higher levels of economic, educational and cultural development never before experienced and not often envisioned. Given a few years of such economic enrichment, we can not only solve the housing situation and eliminate all slums, but we can also eliminate and even reverse the decay of our central cities, as well as replace the rural slums with housing, recreation, sports and other leisure-time facilities befitting our rich nation.

It could permit programs to relieve the distress that daily plagues each of us. We can reopen day-care centers. We can provide decent education and reduce classroom size. We can re-establish free education in city and state universities. We can open the closed hospitals, mental institutions and other needed medical facilities. We can begin to treat our aged with the decency and dignity that they have earned by a lifetime of work for society. We can reduce transportation fares, re-institute the frequency of operation of buses and subways, even clean up the subways and build new ones. We can build highways, rebuild railroads, fill up potholes and repave the pock-marked streets. We can rebuild the collapsed West Side Highway and its counterparts in other cities, and paint and maintain the steel structures so as to prevent their future collapse.

We can build sorely needed garbage incinerators and sewage-treatment plants, and stop that contribution to pollution. We can clean up the Hudson River, the dead Lake Erie, the other dying Great Lakes, as well as the rivers and lakes and streams that befoul our environment. We can even find antipollution methods for waste disposal before the oceans become dead and the air becomes totally unbreathable.

Full employment would reduce sharply the economic causes of racism and allow a human exchange that, given time, could permit us to see each other as people, not as antagonists, competitors, adversaries—and certainly not by the color of our skins, our mode of dress or speech nor by any other superficial and meaningless criteria.

Here, then, is the summary of our Budget of Available Funds, organized and tabulated according to the categories listed on page 91.

The Budget

Amount of available funds

Category #1

1   *Identifiable, realistic amounts that can be saved*

p.		trillions	billions	millions	thousands
p. 96	Secretary of the Treasury Simon's estimate of increase in tax revenues resulting from the elimination of tax shelters		50		
p. 95	A 25% cut in the defense budget		28		
p. 95	Cutting in half the National Intelligence budget		2		
p. 95	Military portion of Foreign Aid 1976		2		
p. 95	One-half portion of budget marked International Affairs		2	300	
p. 96	One-half of 1975 Space budget which probably will be the same in subsequent years		2	450	
p. 96	For the 244 persons with incomes in excess of $200,000 who paid no Federal income tax in 1974, taxes should have been at least			60	
p. 96	Effective rate of corporate income tax reduced from 22.7% in 1967 to 14.5% in 1975—if restored to 1967 level of 22.7%, would yield approximately		6	400	
p. 99	If corporate taxes were paid at the full legal rate of 48% of net profit, the amount of taxes due on $82 billion of profits would be $39.36 billion. This would add ($39.36 billion, minus the previous item, $6.4 billion)		32	960	

Amount of available funds

Category #1 (continued)

	trillions	billions	millions	thousands
p. 101 Federal Trade Commission estimated that consumers have been bilked out of		80		
p. 97 New Towns Program Total loss—Gananda project			21	
Sponsors' defaulted interest payments picked up by HUD			11	
p. 102 New York State taxes on banks, avoided by calling profits by another name			85	
p. 103 New York Telephone Company tax avoidance			120	
p. 103 A 1% tax on the income-yielding assets of New York State banks, insurance and other financial institutions would yield at least		2		
p. 102 New York State part-time jobs at $30,000 per year —if properly paid for— guesstimate				500
p. 102 Moving New York State offices from World Trade Center— savings			4	200
p. 102 Lulus for New York State legislators				880
p. 102 New York State noninterest-bearing accounts—if transferred to earn 5% interest —guesstimate				750
p. 106 Municipal Loan "give-away" program—acknowleged and expected capital loss			70	
p. 107 New York City delinquent real estate taxes, water and sewer charges		1		300

Amount of available funds

				trillions	billions	millions	thousands

Category #1 (continued)

p. 107   New York City granting the real estate tax-assessment reduction to giant corporations — **20** (millions)

p. 108   New York City sale of $900 million of Mitchell-Lama mortgages to private banks and real estate—loss approximately — **250** (millions)

p. 108   New York City losses by Park Department in handing out concessions at "favored" rates — **2** (millions)

p. 106   New York City: If real estate taxes were restored to the same proportion of the city budget as it was in 1915 (78% rather than 23% in 1974), it would result in a minimum of additional taxes of — **4** (billions)

p. 109   New York City Councilman Robert Wagner, Jr.'s estimate of the leasing of unnecessary space — **155** (millions)

p. 109   New York City's removal of 8% "enticement" discount for payment of real estate taxes—guesstimate — **1** (millions)

p. 110   New York City tax on nongovernmental real estate properties now exempt—conservative estimate — **300** (millions)

p. 110   New York City tax on privately owned real estate at its full value (rather than 60% of it) — **1** (billions) **500** (millions)

p. 112   Day-Care Lease fraud, conservative guesstimate — **300** (millions)

Amount of available funds

	trillions	billions	millions	thousands
Category #1 (continued)				
p. 113 Free School-Lunch Program fraud—estimate of fraud in New York State			25	
Category 1. Total		216	336	330

Category #2

Where amounts are regional or not specific, we project a low and conservative figure for the nation as a whole, or the specific entity.

	trillions	billions	millions	thousands
p. 97 Guesstimate of Section 235 default			250	
p. 108 Guesstimate of additional available real estate taxes in New York City by voiding tax-abatement programs for commercial and industrial property, including J-51, etc., x average of 10 years (Trump Organization at Hotel Commodore alone will cost $100 million)			250	
p. 112 Medicaid mill fraud—guesstimate of fraud within the $17 billion national program		2	500	
p. 113 Nursing-home scandal fraud guesstimate (New York State only)			100	
Category 2. Total		3	100	

Amount of available funds

	trillions	*billions*	*millions*	*thousands*
Category #3				
3 *Savings resulting from the reduction of interest rates to a realistic and economically viable 3%.*				
p. 94 Reducing the guesstimate of 6% interest paid on $3 trillion of debt, which is approximately $180 billion, to a rate of 3%. Savings		90		
p. 104 New York City debt service is $2.3 billion. If interest rates are reduced to 3%, savings would be at least		1		
p. 80 FHA insured mortgage debt from 1970 to 1973 = approximately $46 billion. Reduction of interest rate from the current rates to 3% = approximate savings of		2	300	
Category 3. Total		93	300	
Category #4				
4 *Recapture of over-speculated land and real estate values and the inflation causing corporate profit spree.*				
p. 93 Recapture of over-speculated land for the 7 (or 10) year period prior to 1971	1	750		
p. 99 Reducing the record-breaking after-tax corporate profits by only 25%		20	700	
p. 99 Taxes that should have been paid by 8 companies that paid no Federal corporate income taxes in 1974			405	120

Amount of available funds

	trillions	billions	millions	thousands
Category #4 (continued)				
p. 100 Additional income taxes that should have been paid by 8 companies		2	280	
p. 103 Recapture of facilities paid from taxes, given to Con Edison free			500	
p. 104 Worthless land sold to investors in State of Arizona			500	
Category 4. Total	1	774	385	120
Category #5				
5 *Wealth created by putting the unemployed to work.*				
p. 116 With full employment the annual addition to the national wealth is		393	750	
Category 5. Total		393	750	
Category #6				
6 *Wasted funds that cannot easily be recaptured but which indicate that funds can be raised, where there is a desire to do so.*				
p. 95 Elimination of the "overkill" B-1 supersonic bomber program		21	400	
p. 95 Elimination of the new ICBM		30		
p. 95 Estimated cost of Vietnam War to 1973		111	600	
p. 97 Cost to Treasury of contemplated reduction from 70% to 50%, tax bracket for upper-income people, conservative estimate		10		

Amount of available funds

		trillions	billions	millions	thousands
Category #6 (continued)					
p. 96	U.S. Space program, 1960-1975		78	600	
p. 98	Law Enforcement Assistance Administration waste		4		
p. 102	Waste in construction of Albany Mall over and above original estimate			750	
p. 108	New York City cost overrun on Third Water Tunnel			284	
p. 108	New York City Yankee Stadium cost overrun			72	
	Category 6. Total		256	706	
Recapitulation					
Category #1	Identifiable		216	336	330
" #2	Regional		3	100	000
" #3	Interest rates from 6 to 3%		93	300	000
" #4	Recapture	1	774	385	120
" #5	Unemployed		393	750	000
" #6	Wasted funds		256	706	000
	Grand total	2	737	577	450

This budget of Available Funds is only a token budget of what is really available. To be sure, it shows 2 trillion 737 billions of dollars. This figure alone is more than 27 times the $100 billion required to finance our national housing needs. There is enough left over for everything else needed to turn our country around from the disaster course on which we are so rapidly moving.

Some facts regarding this budget need clarification.

The budget is only semi-accurate, in that it contains a mixture of some figures that are one-shot, nonrecurrent amounts, while others recur annually. An example of the former is the recapture of overspeculated land and real estate values. Some examples of the latter are the tax on corporate profits at the full legal level of 48%, the cutting of interest rates to 3% and the money generated by full employment.

Additionally, many billions, and perhaps trillions would be added to the budget, if we were to extend to a national level the wastes, fraud and corruption, which are weighted so heavily on New York City and New York State. Also, our listing of these illegalities hardly scratches the surface. The items are selective and are intended merely as typical reminders of what each of us has read endless times over in the press.

A housing program of the sort projected herein cannot be completed in one year. It would, in all likelihood, take five or even more years. Therefore, the ratio of the token budget of available funds would be multiplied five or ten times over, if the available funds were correlated to the amounts spent annually for housing.

Chapter V

CONCLUSION

The preceding pages contain eloquent facts. But facts alone will not usher in the vital changes that are needed. The powerful forces of the status quo will give us nothing except that which our own united strength can compel.

We need strong, united organizations locally and nationally, organizations of people with clear minds and strong wills and without illusions. Such organizations are easier to bring into existence when we have the facts with which to dispel the myths and lies of landlord/banking propaganda that have bombarded us for long years.

Of course we will be attacked. We will be denounced and ridiculed. Every device to undermine us and divide us will be employed. This is the classic response to any movement of people in defense of their rights. What else but divide and confuse in order to conquer?

When the Congress of Industrial Organizations (C.I.O.) was formed to organize the unorganized in the 1930's, in response to the devastating poverty and unemployment of the Great Depression, the defenders of the status quo responded in just that way. The same nay-sayers cried "creeping socialism" at the entire New Deal of F.D.R. Unemployment Insurance, Social Security, the Wagner Labor Relations Act and Public Housing were considered subversive and would bring doom upon our country.

We need hardly argue that the status quo defenders were both inaccurate and insincere. Yet these same forces were silent and in complete agreement when, for example, the milked-dry subway system in New York City was taken over by the government and paid for in tax-exempt bonds at prices far beyond their value. But the profitability of housing has not yet decayed to that extent, so the anguished cries of the landlord/bankers are to be expected—and disregarded.

As housing comes into the public domain, we must not repeat the errors of the previous experiences. We must not further enrich the landlord/bankers by buying them out, nor should we employ them as "experts" to run housing. They would run it for their own ends and mismanage it in order both to discredit the concept of Housing in the Public Domain in people's eyes, and to reap their own hidden rewards. No, this time housing must be run by and for tenants.

If Housing in the Public Domain seems either radical or impossible, it is no different from any other major social change that history has brought about. The important thing to remember is that it is quite inevitable.

The American people will not continue to watch their cities collapse, their housing decay and their rents rise beyond economic endurance while the population increases and the housing stock diminishes, without taking the inevitable course of action outlined herein. It is in our best tradition. It will gain ever wider acceptance. It will become a fact of life as did other historic advances.

Appendix I

Metropolitan Council on Housing

24 West 30th Street
New York, N.Y. 10001
725-4800

LEGISLATIVE MEMORANDUM

MBR (Maximum Base Rent)

The Maximum Base Rent provision is an amendment to the New York City rent control law. Adopted in 1970, it allows, beginning in 1972, annual 7½% increases in rent with no prospect of reaching an ultimate ceiling, because the ceiling may be raised every two years. The law, according to the city administration, was not intended to benefit landlords per se, but to improve the New York City housing stock. The MBR was to give landlords a "fair" return on their investment, so that they could preserve and improve the housing by making needed repairs. Because a building was supposed to be free of major violations for the annual increase to be issued, landlords, it was hoped, would immediately bring their buildings up to code standards. As Metropolitan Council on Housing predicted when the law passed the City Council, this has proven to be a bitter farce.

The landlord is first granted his increase and then the tenant may file a protest. The rent office is so overburdened that it cannot process the protests even now that two years have passed since the 1972 MBR orders were issued. The result is that many tenants are required under the law to pay the increases despite the existence of violations in their apartments and buildings. The only alternative is to move; with vacancy decontrol, that is not a meaningful alternative. Met Council has numerous documented situations where tenants are living in deplorable conditions, and paying yearly increases nonetheless. Many of these buildings have organized and are now on rent strike.

The MBR was supposed to improve the housing stock. Instead, the additional rent monies are going into the landlords' pockets. The Stein Commission has shown that major renovations and repairs for New York City apartments have decreased since 1970. So much for the unrealistic "hopes" of the City Council that passed the MBR law!

It has been repeated *ad nauseam* that landlords are making huge profits. Yet the constant wails of the landlords (who manage to get a good press to weep in) have given the impression that, for them poverty and bankruptcy are around the corner. With the above in mind, let us examine *just one aspect* of landlord economics. Other aspects—as carefully dissected—will reveal equal horrors.

The MBR law conveys the impression that the landlord is guaranteed "only" an 8.5% annual return on his investment. That is not true. Let us take as an example a landlord who buys a building for $1,000,000. His cash investment is 10% (sometimes only 5%) of the purchase price, in this case, $100,000. Under the old Rent Control Law, before MBR, the landlord was guaranteed an annual return of 6% of the assessed valuation and 2% for depreciation. The assessed value is approximately 60% of the market value.

In our example it breaks down approximately as follows:

Land	$240,000
Building	360,000
Total Assessed Value	$600,000

Under the old Rent Control law the landlord was entitled to a net return of $43,200, which was arrived at as follows:

Total Assessed Value	$600,000	
	x 6%	
		$ 36,000
Building Assessed Value	$360,000	
x 2% Depreciation	x 2%	
		$ 7,200
Guaranteed annual profit		$ 43,200

Under the *MBR formula* the landlord is guaranteed 8.5% of the *equalized assessed valuation*. This EAV, as it is called, is intended to approximate the market value on a county-wide basis. It is arrived at by dividing the assessed value by a county-wide figure determined by the State of New York. In New York City, EAV varies from 45% in Richmond to 65% in Manhattan. The city-wide rate is 57%. Here is what happens when we base the landlord's guaranteed profits upon the EAV:

Total Assessed Value	$600,000
÷ City-wide Rate of 57%	$1,050,631 = EAV
MBR Guaranteed Profit Rate	x .085
(built into the MBR rent formula)	
Total Annual MBR Guaranteed Profit	$ 89,474

Note that the profit has more than doubled. The landlord's actual annual *guaranteed profit* under the MBR becomes *14.9% (in 1975– 15.1%) of the assessed value*, instead of 6% + 2%.

Even these examples do not tell the whole story. By any business standard, profits are measured by actual cash investment—8.5% of the actual cash investment of $100,000 is $8,500.

In the above case the landlord has received more than ten times that amount. His real *guaranteed annual profit is a whopping 89% of his cash investment!* In one year and two months the landlord will have had returned to him his entire capital investment and still own a property yielding guaranteed exorbitant and fantastic profits.

The City Council, at long last realizing that the MBR law is an economic disaster for tenants, repealed it. Attorneys for the landlords, however, brought suit against the city for this action, claiming that the repeal was in violation of the Urstadt Law. Metropolitan Council on Housing was granted permission to intervene on behalf of tenants. The lower courts ruled in favor of the landlords and the higher courts upheld that decision.

The Legislature has the opportunity and the duty to remedy this economic atrocity by the simple expedient of repealing the Urstadt Law, so that the City Council's repeal of the MBR law may become effective.

February 21, 1974 (Revised September 13, 1976)

Appendix II

MANHATTAN PLAZA

Depreciation schedule based on "Double Declining Balances"
showing time required by Lauder/Cohen to recover entire investment

	Annual basis for depreciation	(See Note #1) Amount of depreciation @ 5% per annum	Lauder/Cohen share=20% of amount of depreciation	Lauder/Cohen share of cash flow income from project=20%	Net depreciation after deduction of cash flow income available to Lauder/Cohen (20%)	Savings to Lauder/Cohen @ income tax rate of 70%
Year #1	$95,000,000	4,750,000	950,000	60,000	890,000	623,000
2	90,250,000	4,512,500	902,500	60,000	842,500	589,750
3	85,737,500	4,286,875	857,375	60,000	797,375	558,162
4	81,450,625	4,072,531	814,506	60,000	750,506	525,354
						$2,296,266

Net amount of depreciation savings to Lauder/Cohen in just 4 years (see Note #2)

From here on out all is profit. The table continues as an indication of how double declining balances work. In 13 years, more than 50% of the total depreciation will have been consumed.

	Annual basis for depreciation	Amount of depreciation @ 5% per annum	Lauder/Cohen share=20% of amount of depreciation	Lauder/Cohen share of cash flow income from project=20%	Net depreciation after deduction of cash flow income available to Lauder/Cohen (20%)	Savings to Lauder/Cohen @ income tax rate of 70%
5	77,378,094	3,868,905	773,781	60,000	713,781	499,646
6	73,509,189	3,675,459	735,092	60,000	675,092	472,564
7	69,833,730	3,491,686	698,337	60,000	630,337	441,236
8	66,342,043	3,317,102	663,420	60,000	603,420	422,394
9	63,024,941	3,151,247	630,337	60,000	573,337	401,336
10	59,873,694	2,993,685	598,737	60,000	538,737	377,116

Total depreciation in 10 years $4,910,558

to 40 years in ever diminishing amounts

Note #1   Depreciation over 40 years equals 2½% per year. However, the law allows "double declining balances." Therefore, the rate of depreciation becomes 5% per annum.

Note #2   To this $2,296,266 must be added $240,000 of cash flow income from operations (4 years @ $60,000 per year), bringing their total net income to $2,536,266—or $136,266 more than their entire investment.

The Metropolitan Council on Housing is a New York City-wide tenant union founded in 1958. It has branches and affiliates in many communities of the city. It is almost completely volunteer with a few paid organizers who, together with volunteer organizers, bring tenants together to fight for decent, integrated housing at rents people can afford.

Met Council is a membership organization, funded only by its membership's dues and some modest contributions.

Design by Anthea Lingeman
Cover design and graphics by Michael Perpich
Edited by Irving Kohn
Copy edited by Nan Braymer
Front cover photo by Peter K. Hawley
Back cover photo by Mark Klamkin